D0286637

Breaking Free: Leading the Way

Learning First to Lead Yourself

Traci Duez

2012

Breaking Free: Leading the Way

Copyright © 2012 by Traci Duez

All rights reserved. No part of this book may be reproduced or transmitted in any form or by any means without written permission of the author.

ISBN 978-0-9839901-0-9

Dedication

To everyone who, after my presentations and workshops, asked me...

"Have you written any books on this topic?"

"I wish my son, daughter, husband, wife, boss, co-workers had been here to hear this message."

"Where can I read more about your presentation topic?"

It is to all of you that I dedicate this first book, *Breaking Free: Leading the Way*. This is the first in the Breaking Free series. Thank you!

Table of Contents

Let's Get Started

INTRODUCTION

This book is designed to help you escape some of your old thinking habits that are no longer supporting you and your success by giving you practical, actionable steps to create new habits. This isn't about change; it is about shifting your thinking from using the no longer useful valuing habits to using your natural strengths.

This book won't tell you about some "secret" or magic way of changing. It won't promise you a pain-free route to your success and all of your dreams. It will help you to realize that you are extremely capable of attaining your dreams by using the incredible strengths that you already have.

You are infinitely valuable. Don't believe it? We'll also talk about that in this book and my hope is that you will discover this freeing truth.

It's OK to skip around and find what speaks to you right now. I have tried to structure the book so that you can also read straight through it. I hope to take you on a journey using a variety of stories to help you become a better you.

In my speaking engagements, I encourage the audience to think along with me. Many believe that my talks are "interactive", yet I'm the only one talking. I've tried to make this book interactive in the same way. I hope to be with you on your journey to guide you to new and greater accomplishments that bring peace and joy to your life and career.

My hope is that you read this book over and over; that you buy it for others; that the stories become part of your stories that you share with others.

As I usually offer at the end of my talks, you will have the opportunity to try a free online assessment. I'm hoping that you will take it and that you will then see the value in actually applying your results in your life.

If you have comments, I would love to hear from you. Please send an email to me at *comments@BreakingFreeBooks.com*. You can also sign up for my free monthly newsletter at http://www.breakfreeconsulting.com.

CLAIMING YOUR FREEDOM

I originally wrote this around the United States' 4th of July Independence Day Celebration. The event got me to thinking about our personal freedoms and how precious this gift is to us. But how many of us that live in free countries actually take advantage of that freedom?

As I speak to many people all over the globe, I am realizing that it is often times the individual who chooses to keep themselves bound by not making good choices or knowing that they have choices to make.

Let's look at your last performance review. If it is like most reviews, your supervisor will sit down with you and go over the areas of improvement. Sure, some will tell you what they think you are doing well, but in the end, your development plan will be based upon your weaknesses and how to fix or improve them.

"DOWN ON THE FARM"

If you'll bear with me, I have a short story I'd like to tell you. There once was this puppy named Sparky who was born on a large, beautiful farm. There were acres and acres of fields, a forest with trees and large rocks, a stream that flowed through the pastures, a large barn and farmhouse... everything you'd want on a farm.

As the puppy grew up, she was encouraged to explore the different areas of the farm. At first, Sparky wasn't allowed to stray too far from the farmhouse and barn, but later she had the full run of farm grounds. It was fantastic! She was free! Free to explore and grow, run and jump, climb and dig. She learned a lot of excellent dog skills and was a natural at many of them. Then, her owners taught her how to catch balls and Frisbees. She became a fine retriever as she learned how to "mark" (watch for falling targets that she will later retrieve) and perform blind retrieves (where she has to rely on her owner to tell her where the target is located using a whistle and hand signals). She sure was good at this...

maybe even one of the best. Retrieving made her happy; she seemed passionate about it. She was successful, still free to roam all over the farm, and loved to watch her owners take pride in her abilities.

Then, one day, Sparky's cousin pointed out that there was a fence that went all the way around the farm. He told her that if she really wanted to be successful, she'd find a way to get to the other side of the fence. For the first time, Sparky noticed the fence that went all the way around her incredible farm. It seemed to go on forever. Hmmm, she wondered... what was this? A barrier? Sparky became engrossed in the fence. Instead of practicing her retrieving and other skills, she would run off every morning and look for ways to get over, under or around the fence. She studied the fence (would've taken classes on the fence if she wasn't a dog.) She spent days trying to jump over it... weeks, trying to dig under it... months, trying to run around it. She didn't want to retrieve any more as she was determined to overcome this obstacle. Finally after years of trying, when she couldn't find a way to triumph over the fence, she resigned herself to being an old farm dog. She didn't even want to retrieve any more. And retrieving just didn't seem to be as fun, especially knowing that she failed at overcoming the fence.

FREEDOM IS IN YOUR STRENGTHS

Does your life experience sound a little like Sparky's? How often do you focus on what you can't do? Do you obsessively look for problems that you need to fix? How often do you allow others to set your expectations and define your goals?

I meet so many people who are shackled by their weaknesses. Their thinking habits are wrapped up in overcoming these "barriers" and rectifying their shortcomings. They set expectations around overcoming their weaknesses and fixing their problems. They forget to play to their strengths and look for opportunities to succeed doing what they really like to do (and are really good at doing).

Do you have the expectation that "I can do anything" which is usually followed by the implication that "I can do anything and be successful at it"? I know my grandfather told me that I could do anything when I was younger. Sure it sounds good, but it's not the truth. I can't be successful at anything and neither can you. (That doesn't sound like something a coach and motivational speaker should say, right?) But it is the truth.

I can't win American Idol; I'm not going to win an Olympic medal in artistic gymnastics; I'm not going to be the next Food Network Star. I cannot do *anything* and be successful at it. I could try and try to learn how to sing. I could spend years and boatloads of money on a singing coach and a performance coach and an image consultant. But my chances of winning would still be zero--I can't and won't sing well (as this isn't one of my talents) and I'm too old to be eligible anyway.

But I can do *something*! **You can do something too!!** *What are your strengths?* When I ask people that question there is often a full minute or more of silence. So I ask you, *what are your strengths?*

Write them down on a scrap of paper. Go ahead, take a few minutes, I'll wait.

Now, what are your weaknesses? Do those thoughts pop into your mind almost immediately? They do for most of the people I talk with.

Your brain readily retrieves the thoughts that you focus on the most. If your weaknesses come to mind faster than your strengths, you may be spending your time trying to get over, under or around your fences. **Stop it!** Turn around. There is a vast field of opportunity for you. It's right there in front of you. It is your strengths... your natural gifts and blessings. Start to focus on them and you will soon find freedom and joy and peace and happiness in your life and in your career.

1) **Look for your strengths**

    If you can't figure out what they are because you have focused on your weaknesses for so long, ask a friend, family or colleague for help. Even though your mind may disagree with them, give them the benefit of the doubt. Many times they know your strengths better than you do.

2) **Ignore your weaknesses**

What you think about most is what your brain turns into your habits. If you are focusing on your weaknesses, even to *FIX* them, you are actually training your brain that you want to make your weaknesses stronger so that your weaknesses will have more of an impact on your life because they will become stronger habits.

3) **Take an assessment**

There are many assessments available. You can even find a link to one in the Reference section of this book. Your report will show you how to use your strength immediately.

4) **Look for ways to strengthen your strengths**

Start with your dominant talent. Then add skills, knowledge, and practice to the mix. Building on your strength will also help you to find your passion. Our coaching program teaches you the skills, the knowledge, and gives you the practice that you need to ignore the thoughts that are getting in your way. Our coaching (neuro-axiology) helps you go into your mind to shift to a more balanced and productive thought. We help you to scientifically strengthen your strengths!

5) **Help others to see their strengths**

Develop the habit of strengths-finding in yourself and in others! By helping others around you know and understand their strengths, you will become more successful... your team will become more successful. If you're a leader, don't try to get your team members to overcome their weaknesses, send them to training and workshops that focuses on their strengths... assign them tasks that are aligned with their strengths. You will be amazed at the progress you make when you take this approach.

I'd like to finish with a story from Mark Twain. He described a man who died and met St. Peter at the gates of heaven. Knowing that St. Peter was wise and met all of the souls that passed this way, the man asked St. Peter a question.

He said, "I've studied military history for most of my life. So, can you tell me, who was the greatest general of all time?"

St. Peter responded quickly saying, "That's easy. It's that man over there."

"You must be mistaken," the man responded, "I knew that guy on earth and he wasn't a general. He was just a common laborer."

"That's right my friend," assured St. Peter. "He would've been the greatest general of all time if he had been a general."

What is your greatest strength? *Claim it today!* Every human being has talents and strengths that they were given at birth. These strengths are what lead you to feeling and experiencing freedom. Are you developing yours? Do you know what gifts you were given? Your strengths are just waiting to be uncovered. If you'll allow me, I would love to help.

Section 1

The Basics

Basic Axiology

I will be referencing a lot of axiology in this book so I wanted to give you a brief overview of the science. This will provide a basis for most of the articles in this book.

Robert S. Hartman

Robert S. Hartman is the father of formal axiology. He was born in Berlin Germany on January 27, 1910. He had an interest in politics and economics from an early age. He attended the German College of Political Science, the University of Paris, the London School of Economics, and Berlin University, where he received the LL.B. in 1932. As he was growing up, he was able to see that what the Nazi's were doing was wrong. He rejected the creeds of Communism, Nazism, and Fascism which he expressed in his speeches and writings. Using a fake passport, he left Germany in 1932 for England. Because of his outspokenness against Nazism, the Nazis attempted to keep track of him. He changed his name (Robert Schirokauer) legally to that on the passport, Robert S. (for Schirokauer) Hartman.

It was somewhere during these years that Robert Hartman developed his personal mission in life: "To organize good the way that he saw Hitler organize evil." Isn't that a powerful mission statement?

In order to pursue this mission, he immigrated to the United States where he studied mathematics and received a doctoral degree in philosophy from Northwestern University in 1946. He held more than fifty lectureships in the United States, Canada, Latin America, and Europe. He was a research professor of philosophy at the National University of Mexico from 1957, and at the University of Tennessee from 1968 until his death in 1973.

Why am I telling you this? Because axiology will make more sense in this context. You see, Dr. Hartman's life-long quest was to figure out the first part of his mission statement. He needed to answer the question, "What is good?" And to answer the question in such a way that good could be organized to help preserve and enhance the value of human life. He believed that he had found this answer in the axiom upon which he based his science of Axiology, "A thing is good when it fulfills its concept." If you'd like, you can learn more about this concept in his major work, *The Structure of Value: Foundations of Scientific Axiology* (1967).

He was very practical not just theoretical. His extensive work in promoting profit sharing became the basis for today's 401k retirement savings plans.

AXIOLOGY THE SCIENCE

You may ask, "I've never heard of axiology. How long has it been around?" Well, that's understandable as axiology (value science) has only existed as a philosophy for over 2500 years: since the time of Plato and Socrates. However, it was not until the mid-1900s that it evolved into a formal science.

Axiology gets its name from the Greek words, *axios*, meaning "value" or "worth," and logos, meaning "science."

THREE DIMENSIONS OF VALUE

Hartman was the first to come up with the concept of the three dimensions of value. (In the past, most other philosophers had considered two dimensions—extrinsic and systemic.) Everything can be classified in to these three dimensions and these three dimensions have relative value to one another.

Let's start with the lowest class of value... Systemic. Systemic values exist only mentally, but all of us can use them to order chaos. Systemic entities can be defined with absolute precision in only a few words, and every true instance of them is flawless. A circle that deviates slightly from being "a closed curved line with no thickness at all, every point of which is equally distant from its center" is not really a circle. With the systemic dimension we have black and white thinking, rules, procedures, policies, perfection and anything that is part of a system. As with rules, you are either adhering to the parameters of the rule or you are not. In the mathematics of axiology, we can think of systemic as binary. It's either a 1 or a 0.

The next dimension of value in the hierarchy of value is Extrinsic. Extrinsic value is exponentially more valuable than systemic because now you are taking a system, an idea, a concept and using it to create something measurable and tangible. With extrinsic value, things can be put into classes or categories. Things can be judged not simply as right or wrong (as with systemic) but as good, better and best. Mathematically speaking, the extrinsic dimension is a finite number or n. {This definition is putting it very simply. The actual mathematics of axiology uses set theory and the extrinsic dimension is signified by $\varkappa_0$ (aleph-naught)}.

The highest dimension of value is Intrinsic. Intrinsic value deals with personal or spiritual value. Intrinsic has an infinite number of properties or value which can be defined in an infinite number of ways. The value of a person is infinite, irreplaceable, and priceless. The 'thing' itself is valued for its own unique individuality. Mathematically speaking, we can symbolize this with infinity (∞). {Again using set theory, the actual symbol for non-denumerably infinite is $\varkappa_1$ (aleph-one)}.

To give you an example going up the hierarchy of value, we use the creation of a cell phone. At the lowest (least valuable) stage, someone had an idea that portable phones would be good. The idea is wonderful, just like a time travel machine at this stage, but it has no real tangible value. Even if a plan was put together on all of the pieces and parts that were needed to put the cell phone together, it still doesn't exist. (These plans and ideas fall into the systemic dimension.) So when folks start to execute the plan and start putting the pieces of the cell phone together, they are moving from the systemic dimension of value to the exponentially more valuable extrinsic dimension of value.

For many of us, that's about all that we see. However, as Hartman showed us, there is a dimension of value that is infinitely more valuable than the systemic and extrinsic combined. When does the cell phone have intrinsic (infinite) value? When there has been an accident and a cell phone can be used to call for help and save lives. Now the extrinsic cell phone has intrinsic (infinite) value. Without it, infinitely valuable human beings would be lost.

THE HARTMAN VALUE PROFILE

Axiology, the science of human value and value judgments, enables us to identify the internal valuing systems that influence our perceptions, decisions and actions - to clearly understand "why" we do what we do.

The Hartman Value Profile (HVP) is the tool that allows us to do that. The HVP measures a person's capacity to make value judgments concerning the world and one's self. It consists of two parts: Part 1 is a list of 18 items pertaining to the world, and part 2 consists of 18 phrases related to the self.

To complete the HVP, a person is asked to rank the items in Part 1 from best to worst and the phrases in Part 2 from most agree to least agree. The results reflect an individual's own preferences, or their own personal hierarchy of value, which are measured against the objective, mathematical scale given by formal axiology. This measurement is very precise.

If you would like to try this assessment for free, please go to the Reference section of this book for instructions.

SUMMARY

Intrinsic	>	Extrinsic	>	Systemic
People	>	Things	>	Ideas
∞	>	n	>	1
$\aleph_1$	>	$\aleph_0$	>	1

YOU ARE NOT WHAT YOU THINK

OK, read the title again... You are *NOT* what you think.

- Does it sound like an incomplete sentence?
- Is your first reaction to be offended? (Who does she think she is saying that to me?!)
- Is your first thought to say "Thank goodness!" (I'd hate to be what I think.)
- Are you simply asking "Who cares??"

Studies show that 95% of our population cannot separate their ideas from their self-worth. Many folks believe that if you don't like their *IDEA*, you don't like them.

We're going to explore that a little further by having you look at:

- What you think and
- How you react when someone challenges what you think.

YOU ARE NOT YOUR THOUGHTS

What I'm trying to stress when I say, "You are not what you think" is that you are not your thoughts.

- When someone criticizes your thinking, ideas, expectations or approach, do your thoughts tell you that they are devaluing *YOU*?
- Do you look at opposing ideas with an open mind or are you busy defending your own ideas?
- Do you listen to the ideas of others or is your mind busy planning what you're going to say next?

Your thoughts may drive your current feelings, emotions, choices, actions and ultimately the results you are creating in your life, but your thoughts are not *YOU*. Your thoughts may control your attitude, your personality, your behavior, but your thoughts, still, are not you. *YOU are the one who can control your thoughts!* That person, the one in control, is the *REAL YOU!*

YOU HAVE A CHOICE

Are you conscious of your choice to act upon or believe your thoughts OR are you a victim of your thought habits and internal dialogue?

Many people go through life bound by choices that were made for them which they simply accepted and turned into thought habits. Many are constrained by choices that were made without any conscious thought on their part. "It's just the way it is." "That's the way I've always been."

It doesn't HAVE TO be that way!

THE SCIENCE

Your brain likes to conserve energy. It does this by moving frequent thoughts into your habit center. Conscious thought uses far more energy than habitual thought. For instance, think about driving your car here in the US. If you live here, you probably know how to do that almost unconsciously. Now, think about driving a car in England or Jamaica where they drive on the left (or as some would say, wrong) side of the road. Your brain will have to use a lot more energy to help your body steer the car and keep it going in the right direction.

Some studies suggest that the average person thinks between 12,000 and 50,000 thoughts per day. These studies also suggest that over 90% of these thoughts were the same thoughts you thought yesterday and are getting pushed deeper and deeper into your habit center. Your thoughts will actually begin to make you think that you ARE a certain way and that there is NO other choice... unless YOU, the real YOU, take back the control.

THE SOLUTION

Step 1: <u>Learn to recognize when you are attached and holding on tightly to your thoughts and ideas</u>.

Become part of the 5%. The 5% of our population who are confident in who they are and who realize they are not their ideas!

Here are a few things you should consider:

1) When someone criticizes your idea, do you *feel a physiological response*? Do you feel the need to prove that YOU are right? Does the hair stand up on the back of your neck, do your palms perspire, does your heart race?

2) When something goes wrong in your life or not as you'd expected, do you *catastrophize* the criticism by mulling it over in your mind until it becomes larger than life? You will recognize this by the use words like "everything, everyone, no one, never, and always." Do you hear yourself saying things like

   a. "Everything is going wrong!"?

   b. "No one ever supports my decisions."

   c. "This happens every time."?

3) When someone expresses a new idea, do your thoughts immediately go to what's wrong with the idea? Are you *looking for the faults and flaws* in their plan or proposal? Are you always correcting other's documents or spreadsheets?

4) Do you *personalize* the opinions of others? When someone comments on your idea by saying, "That's a stupid idea", does your internal dialogue hear, "You are stupid"?

5) Do you get *frustrated* by the weather, the traffic, other people's performance, your financial condition, relationships, and your job when they don't meet your expectations? What is your response when your ideas and thoughts about what and how things should be are not met? What happens when your expectation does not match reality?

Think about these situations for a minute. Do you recognize these situations in your life?

They are all caused by YOUR thoughts.

If you sense a challenge in this area become aware of your thoughts at the moment you have these feelings and ideas. These are <u>pivotal moments</u>. Are you making a conscious choice at that moment? Or, are you allowing your thought habits to be in control of your response?

Step 2: <u>Learn to detach yourself from your thoughts, ideas and expectations</u>.

As you sense the physiological reaction (heart racing, muscles tensing, palms sweating, etc.), take a second to analyze your thoughts and go back into your mind to find a second thought.

Here's a tip for handling ideas presented by other people that may not match your idea. Before you criticize or comment, say this to them...

"What I like best about your idea is _____."

"Have you considered _____?"

Work to find the good in their idea *FIRST*. Be sure to acknowledge *THEIR* idea not just *THAT* idea using the word "your." Then express your concerns or issues. You will soon find that you are better able to combine ideas and come up with the true, best idea.

Lastly, remember this:

You are *NOT* your thoughts! You are *NOT* your ideas!

You have a choice.

Success is consistently making *CONSCIOUS* choices at the pivotal moments throughout your day.

Section 2

Goals & Direction

THE PRISON OF PERFECTION

As I have asked others what gets in the way of them actually making decisions, one of the overwhelming responses is fear. As I probed a little deeper, I found out that the fear is often caused by perfection.

Many people overvalue the idea of perfection which causes them to devalue reality. The idea ends up having more value in their minds than actually creating and engaging in life. Instead of improving life, perfection creates a prison.

THE WALLS OF PRISON

So what does this perfection prison look like? Well, it only exists in your mind and it can be a major obstacle to your joy and happiness. The retaining bars of your prison are *NOT* real. They only appear real in your imagination. The bars of your prison may be created by:

- **Rejecting Failure.** Refusing to recognize a positive side to failure. For you perfectionists, your initial reaction to that last statement may be disbelief. What good can come of failure? Well, according to neuroscientists a great deal of good can come from failure because our mind is really good at detecting "errors." That is how it creates new thoughts and neuropathways. You need failures to help your brain succeed.
- **Rejecting Success.** Refusing to "lower" your standards of perfection. The pursuit of perfection requires high standards and yet as the perfectionist approaches a high standard they immediately reset to even higher standards thus never celebrating success. By the way, celebrating success is also good for the brain.
- **Rejecting Painful Emotions**. Pain equals not perfect in the mind of the perfectionist. Happiness is the perfectionist's goal and negative emotions fall short of that goal so these are avoided at all costs.

- **Rejecting Positive Emotions.** By consistently and constantly setting goals that will never be reached, the perfectionist, by default, has little to celebrate. Realistically, when will your performance be perfect? Can't you always find something to improve? So, when will perfection be reached? Never.
- **Rejecting the Full Experience of Life.** Life is flawed in the perfectionists mind. Perfection locks you into one specific outcome. The perfectionist spends much time living in their imagination and their "what if" world, missing out on the experience and journey of life.

All of this leads to FEAR (being Fully Engaged in Avoiding Reality).

WHAT IS PERFECTION?

Let's take a closer look at perfection from a number of perspectives...

Axiologically, perfection falls into the systemic category or the lowest axiological class of value. It is an idea, a concept that only exists in the mind or imagination of a human being. What is "perfect" to one person may not be "perfect" to another.

The definition of perfection is imperfect. In most of the definitions on dictionary.com, the world 'perfect' is used to define perfection. When you look up perfect, you find:

- Conforming absolutely to the description or definition of an ideal type
- Entirely without any flaws, defects, or shortcomings
- Excellent or complete beyond practical or theoretical improvement

So, when will a human being ever be "ideal" or "without flaws" or "beyond improvement"? *NEVER!*

Logically, perfection is imperfect. As my mentor, Harvey Schoof says "Perfection is the unrelenting, unyielding pursuit of the unachievable." Perfection isn't real. It's purely imaginary.

THE IMPACT OF PERFECTION

Neuroscience tells us that systemic thoughts occur in the back or "old" part of the brain. This is in the same area as the amygdala. The amygdala is the prehistoric part of your brain that developed to help you in times of danger. It's the fight, flight, or freeze mechanism that shuts down your conscious thoughts when it recognizes an "error" and redirects hormones and energy to your muscles so that you can react quickly to save yourself.

How does this impact you? Well, if your mind overvalues perfection, it will believe that its idea is more valuable than reality. When reality differs from your imagination, it detects an "error" in reality and causes the fight-flight-freeze response. This shuts down your logical, rational thinking brain and redirects energy to your reactionary systems.

There are two main areas where perfection can negatively impact your life: devaluing people and devaluing yourself. Let's take a closer look at both of these areas.

Devaluing People

You have probably seen this misalignment of value or valuing habits in your everyday life. Your Core Values will tell you that people are more important than thoughts or ideas and axiology proves that mathematically. Yet, how many times do you see a parent berating a child who has made a minor mistake? As I umpire Little League baseball games, I see it all the time. A 10 year-old child makes a mistake running the bases and the manager (usually their dad or man in his late 30's or 40's) gets in the child's face and tells him how stupid he is or how he can't do the simplest task. You see, the idea of how the child *SHOULD*

HAVE performed ends up being more important than the child, at that moment.

Misalignment, or as it's called in axiology, this transposition of value, causes a great deal of stress in the lives of people every day. And, it may be causing some children to develop debilitating perfectionistic tendencies as well.

Devaluing Yourself

Some people say that they use perfection to provide them with motivation to achieve more than they would otherwise achieve. They hold this idea in front of them so that they are continuously striving and pushing themselves. That is very logical if goals are reachable, but perfection isn't possible.

The habit that you, the perfectionist, are inadvertently creating is that you are valuing 'perfection', something that is systemic, over things that are extrinsic or even intrinsic. You are creating valuing habits that aren't aligned with your Core Values.

Let's look at this logically. What happens if you "lower your standards" and, say, instead of shooting for the stars, you aim first for the clouds? When you reach the clouds, what will happen?

- You could celebrate your success and achievements (and set up your brain for further success.)
- You could set another goal that takes you further beyond the clouds towards the stars.
- You could reset your goals from your new perspective as you look around from the clouds. I mean, what if the clouds give you nosebleeds and as you look down you find wonderment in the oceans?

Perfection keeps you locked up or locked in on a path and doesn't allow you, the real YOU, to change your mind or make better decisions from your new perspective because it values the idea above your experience.

So, when does perfection *ADD VALUE* to your life? When will you achieve it?

I believe perfection isn't something to strive for; it is your enemy. It doesn't get you closer to your dreams; it drives a wedge between you and your dreams. Focusing on perfection doesn't give us positive emotions. It causes fear, frustration, guilt, discouragement, disillusion, anger, and hesitancy.

STRIVE FOR GREATNESS

So, are you just supposed to "lower your standards?" I'd ask you in return—do you want to advance toward your goals *AND* experience joy? Then, the answer to your question is *YES*! Lower your standards. OK, don't stop reading—I haven't lost it. Let me explain.

Instead of shooting for perfection (i.e., standards that can never be met), shoot for greatness (standards that are beyond where you are now but can be reached). You can always select another standard after you achieve the one you are currently pursuing.

Greatness doesn't cause you to lower your standards. It helps you to map out the steps to achieve your goals while allowing you to be human; allowing you to be flexible, allowing you to celebrate being the unique, priceless and irreplaceable person that you are.

BECOME AN **EXCEL**ERATOR

Instead of being a perfectionist become an EXCELerator. Choose to throw away or discard your perfectionistic thoughts. These thoughts and standards don't add value to your life.

Choose to escape the Perfection Prison by...

1) **Pursuing Excellence**. To excel means to surpass or outdo. It comes from the Latin word *excellare* which means "to rise,

surpass, be eminent." Remember, it's the journey that produces the results.

2) **Compete against yourself.** Many people try to 'excel' past others. I want to encourage you to focus on surpassing the you of yesterday. As Og Mandino writes *"I will climb today's mountain to the utmost of my ability yet tomorrow I will climb higher than today, and the next will be higher than tomorrow. To surpass the deeds of others is unimportant; to surpass my own deeds is all."*

3) **Focus on YOUR Strengths.** Strive to be your best. Appreciate the value in hard work and failure. Failure shows you areas of weaknesses and STRENGTH. It is your strengths that provide the foundation for your growth. Focus on what you're good at and what you like to do.

Act! Remember that fear (unless you're in physical danger) is not real. Another quote from Og Mandino is, *"Now I know that to conquer fear I must always act without hesitation and the flutters in my heart will vanish."* When you focus on your strength, acting without fear is much easier.

OPTICAL DELUSIONS

Often, you hear statements that you perceive are unbelievable. You may even respond by saying, "Are you kidding me?!?" Today, I'd like you to focus on a similar question...

"ARE YOU KIDDING YOU?!?"

Your perception is your reality. But, what if your perception doesn't accurately reflect the current moment? In order to bring intrinsic value to any moment, project, relationship, etc., you need to be aligned with the present reality.

WHAT ARE OPTICAL DELUSIONS?

Well, I think you know what an optical illusion is, right? It's something that appears one way, but is actually another. Like the image to the right... it looks like the bottom line is longer than the top, yet if you measure them, they are exactly the same length.

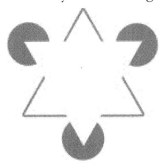

In the picture to the left, how many triangles do you see? Most people will say 2 or 6 or 8. How many are there? *ZERO!* Your brain, however, has been trained to recognize patterns so it 'helps' you and somehow interprets the notches in the circles and the "V" shapes as triangles.

The word 'optical' refers to sight or vision. The word 'illusion' means something that deceives; a false impression or idea. However, the word *delusion* refers to a persistent false belief.

You should recognize in the picture on the left above that there are no triangles present. Even if you once believed the illusions that there were triangles, you should now be able to take a closer look and see that there are none. If you still held on to your belief, this would indicate a delusion.

EXAMPLES OF OPTICAL DELUSIONS

Many times your own mind creates optical delusions that you persistently believe even when evidence appears that demonstrates reality isn't in agreement with your delusion.

As you may know, in my business I assess the way people think and make decisions. Using an axiological assessment, we can measure the pattern of decision-making which the person uses when processing information about the world and themselves. Using the Hartman Value Profile, we do not ask the respondents to describe themselves. Doing this would not yield accurate results if they were "suffering" from optical delusions because they would 'delude' the assessment. The Hartman Value Profile (HVP) places its emphasis upon thinking, not behaving. It allows me to determine the root thinking style that lies at the base of a person's decision-making.

So, I ask my client to go through the process of ranking two sets of eighteen items. From this I will get 36 measurements that indicate how the person typically thinks... the thoughts and internal dialogue that exist within his/her mind. I am sometimes amazed by what some of my clients think and say about their measurements.

Now, as you can imagine, rarely is it possible that every one of your thought processes are perfectly able to see reality as it is. So, you will have a few measurements that are out-of-balance. I have had a couple of clients who didn't or wouldn't recognize this imbalance.

One, for instance, called me after he ranked his 2 sets of 18 items and asked, "Do we still have to meet to discuss my results? I'm pretty sure I put them all in the right order."

Needless to say, my client's view of reality (that he answered the test perfectly) may be a little askew, yet he believes that it is completely and perfectly balanced (even though there were areas of great imbalance). This is an "optical" delusion.

Recently, I also had another client who is in sales. As we talked through her assessment report, she kept telling me, "One thing for sure is that I know sales." "I can sell anything." "I am great at selling." When asked how successful she had been lately, as she had started a new position within the last year, she confessed that she hadn't sold anything yet. The reason for this was not her fault, however. She wasn't handed the 'good' accounts. She didn't have the support that she needed. *Yet*, to her credit, she was going through this assessment to find her 'blind spots.' In the end, though, her mind was much more comfortable holding on to her delusions. These optical delusions will keep her from 'seeing' her blind spots... even though they were clearly laid out in front of her in black, white, yellow and red. I wish I could better help her to step back and see that the only thing getting in the way of her success is the delusions that her mind has created.

YOUR OPTICAL DELUSIONS/BLIND SPOTS

What are the causes of these optical delusions? For the answer to that, let's look at how your brain works.

Neuroscience teaches us about the electro-bio-chemical dynamics of how neuropathways (the brain's highway system of thinking) develop, grow, and mature. As you go through life, your brain "sees" billions and billions of things each and every day. Many times your brain ignores or filters the things that it sees and other times you choose to focus on them.

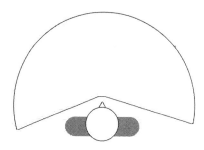

As your brain goes with you throughout your daily life, you are constantly filtering and focusing. Your brain will create neuropathways based upon your focus. Sometimes this produces good, balanced thinking habits... your brain will take in all the information that it can about an observation and then process that information. Your brain has an *uninhibited field of vision.* You do not have any blind spots in this area of thought.

Now, in other situations, you have trained your brain (either consciously or unconsciously) to filter your observations. These filters can come from something as innocuous as your parents saying "Don't talk to strangers." Your brain may have 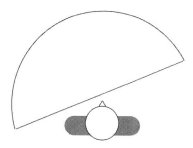 thought about that (focused on it) over-and-over again creating a hardwired neuropathway which now manifests itself as you being distrusting of people you don't know well. Your field of vision has been constricted and *you have a blind spot.*

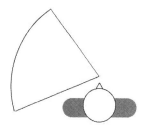

Your blind spot can exist in varying degrees. Instead of just missing a small part of reality in your picture, your brain may actually filter out a large part of the data. At one time, this filtering habit may have been very supportive of your efforts. However, today, it may be the very thing that is keeping you from reaching your goals and having the balance and success in your life that you desire.

CONSIDER THESE THINGS....

Close your left eye and fixate your right eye on the cross in the diagram. If your eye is about 12 inches (30 cm) away, you should notice that the X to the right disappears. (This distance may vary slightly so feel free to slowly move a little closer or farther away.)

Why does this phenomenon happen? Each of your eyes contains an area that has no photoreceptors because it is occupied by the optic nerve. The brain simply "fills in" the most probable stimulus (in this case, a uniform black line) where there is none.

How often does this happen to you when it comes to a situation? Does your brain automatically recognize a pattern and *ASSUME* to know what fills in the unknown areas?

Many times this does happen and *YOU* miss out on opportunities... opportunities to bring Intrinsic (infinite) value to a situation. When you don't take the time to see the "big picture", you are letting the habits of your mind run your life. You have the ability to not only "see" your blind spots as clearly as you see the big X above, but also to correct them through the breakthroughs in neuro-axiology.

STEPS TO REVEAL AND CORRECT YOUR OPTICAL DELUSIONS

You can only bring intrinsic value to your world when you see it clearly. At the risk of superfluous self-promotion, here are some helpful suggestions:

1) Take the *FREE* Assessment that can be found in the Reference section of this book. It only takes about 10-20 minutes to complete online.

2) Review your Results.

3) Schedule a *FREE* consultation by following the instructions that come with your results. We will work together and put them in the context of your life.

4) Use *YOUR* Strengths. Neuroscientifically, it has been proven that 'fixing' your weaknesses is extremely difficult if not impossible. You must learn to focus on your strengths... focus on your uniqueness. These are indicated by the green bars in your assessment. It is your strengths that will help you overcome and eventually eliminate your delusions.

I want to help you reach your goals and your success. Many of the people that I speak with talk about *balance*. When your thought life is balanced (absent of delusions), your life will be balanced. *You can't balance your life without balancing the underlying thoughts that create it.*

Deciding About Indecision

I was trying to decide what to write. At first, nothing exciting came to mind. Then lots of ideas came to my head but after re-evaluating, those ideas might not have been too exciting either.

Then, it happened. I thought that writing about decision making and overcoming indecisiveness would be valuable and maybe even exciting.

The Choices You Make

Let's look at how long it takes you to make a decision.

How much mental energy do you put into deciding:

- Where to eat dinner?
- What clothes to wear?
- Where to go on vacation?
- What product to buy?

How long does it take you to make decisions at work?

- Which resources to use?
- What path to take?
- How much time to invest?

Every choice you make means that you lose out on all of the other options. Choice = loss. Doesn't that seem very final?

Good Decisions

We all want to make good decisions and choices. A choice is a value judgment plain and simple. Choice is about selecting the option that your mind believes is the best decision. It's about what adds the greatest value.

At times, you may question your ability to make good decisions. Why is that? Is it because you weren't taught how to do so? Do you not know what a good decision-making process looks like? Do you overvalue the impact of the decision and not see it (or the options) in proper perspective?

The conclusions you make about the 'right' thing to do are not always accurate. Sometimes your perception or perspective is 'off' or out of focus. This may cause you to be wary of making a decision because past choices may have not met your expectations. Good choices are value-centered!

So how do you make good, *value-centered choices?*

THE NATURAL LAWS OF VALUE

What most people don't realize is that value follows natural laws. Natural laws can be broken like man-made laws with one exception: You can't get away with breaking a natural law.

The science of axiology describes the natural laws and principles of value. When you understand these principles of value, you allow yourself to be surer of your decisions.

AXIOLOGY AND YOUR BRAIN

Sometimes when it comes to making decisions your mind, actually your valuing habits, battle one another and cause you to be indecisive.

Here's what happens in your mind...

As you think, your brain filters and compares. It values some information more than other information. In some cases, your mind can't make up its mind.

I often use axiology (the study of values, valuing and valuations) to identify and explain people's thinking. Axiology tells us that there are three classes of value:

- Intrinsic: infinitely valuable, immeasurable 'things'; people.
- Extrinsic: finitely valuable, measurable things; tangible objects
- Systemic: conceptual things; ideas

Each class has an objective value relative to one another.

Intrinsic > Extrinsic > Systemic

Intrinsically valuable things are always more valuable than Extrinsically valuable things. Extrinsic is always more valuable than Systemic.

Each of these classes of value is processed in a different area of your brain. Your brain likes to conserve energy so as you make a specific value judgment (accurate or not) over and over and over again, your brain creates habits. When this happens, these habits take control and influence your choices.

So what happens if your valuing habits (many that you did not create consciously), aren't congruent with the natural laws of value? What if your valuing habits haven't consistently produced the results that you'd like?

WATCH OUT FOR TRAPS

Depending upon the valuing habits that your mind created, you may fall into certain decision-making traps. Do you recognize any of these?

- <u>Over Analysis</u>: Your mind will require an almost unending stream of data in order to analyze it and make a decision. In most cases, your mind paralyzes itself because the more facts it accumulates, the more facts it still wants in order to get ready to decide.

- <u>Over Anxious</u>: Your mind requires very little information to make a decision. It chooses the information that is directly in front of it... until something else is presented. Then, of course, your mind will choose that one.

- <u>People-Pleasing</u>: Your mind doesn't really focus on the actual decision; it focuses on what other people will think about the decision. So, your mind isn't really doing its own thinking about the choice, but thinking about what other people might be thinking about the choice.

- Procrastinating: Your mind dreads making a final decision so it puts it off as long as possible. It resists taking a stand.

You may also think of other traps but in almost every instance the foundation of the trap is *FEAR*. Fear of failure; Fear of missing out; Fear of being laughed at, etc.

Many of you may have heard that fear is an acronym for *"False Evidence Appearing Real."* I'm not fond of that acronym because it makes us out to be victims. Instead, here is another acronym which better epitomizes my beliefs:

Fully Engaged in Avoiding Reality

(Now, with this definition, you are more in charge of the *fear* and not the victim of some "false evidence appearing real".)

OVERCOMING INDECISION

In order to overcome your indecision, you must overcome your fears. I'm passionate about neuro-axiology because I have used this science/methodology to overcome my fears. (Yes, I was terrified of public speaking and overcame that in under a year.)

When you understand axiology and the hierarchy of value, you are better prepared to know the "right" or "best" decision. For instance, if you know that the law of value teaches that people are more important than things, you are able to pick "caring for a friend" (intrinsic) over "donating to a charity" (extrinsic). You are able to choose "living with integrity" (intrinsic) over "being loyal" (systemic). And, when you make these decisions, you can be sure that they will be "good" decisions.

So, what can you do today to make conscious, deliberate, good choices and overcome indecision?

1) **Stay in the Now.** Learn to use your natural thinking and valuing strengths. (You can do this easily by trying the free assessment link at the end of the book and scheduling a consultation to talk about your results.)

2) **Practice on the little things**. When someone asks you where you want to go for lunch, don't say "I don't care. Where do you want to go?" Check in with your strong valuing habits and decide on a place. Don't worry about the other person's response (that's in the future) or what they'll think or if they like that type of food. That isn't what they asked you. Answer the question! Look at it as practicing for the *BIG* decisions. :)

3) **Act**! Remember decisions without action are fruitless. Some folks spend so much time making the decision that when it comes time to act, it's too late or they have no energy to move forward.

4) **Manage your decisions**. More important than making the decision is managing it! Our brain isn't a computer that has to follow the initial program that was written on its hard drive. Our brains are recreating our hard drives and writing new programs all the time. Even if we make a wrong turn, our brain has the power to direct us and correct us. (Neuro-axiology also teaches us about how to do this as well.)

5) **Learn more about neuro-axiology** (the science of value). The principles and natural laws associated with making good choices are immutable. When you learn to become more value-centered, you will see that the quality of your choices will increase and so will your confidence in making them.

CHOOSE YOUR DIRECTION

For most of us, every New Year brings us to thoughts of New Goals. You don't have to wait for a time on the calendar. Right now, I'd like for you to try a New Approach.

"Experts" will tell you to set clear, defined, measurable goals... short-range, mid-range and long-range goals... and don't forget to put a date on them, a deadline. So you'll list out things like Lose 20 pounds by 3/30; Volunteer at Soup Kitchen by 2/29, Learn to Speak Spanish by 9/30, Take Technical Training Class by 7/31, and Clean Garage by 4/30. Then, as the year goes along, IF you remember, you'll look at these goals and "work on" them. Some goals you might even accomplish.

But, I want to help you bring Intrinsic (infinite) value to who you are and what you do. So, I'm going to ask you to take a new approach this year...

DON'T WRITE DOWN YOUR GOALS!! (yet)

What? That may sound silly coming from someone who professes to be a coach. You may be thinking, "Shouldn't you be helping people to accomplish their goals?" Allow me to explain.

YALE GOALS STUDY NEVER HAPPENED

Have you heard this story told by motivational speakers, coaches and personal development gurus? In the annals of personal goal-setting, no story outranks the Yale University Class of 1953.

The story goes like this: In 1953, researchers surveyed Yale's graduating seniors to determine how many of them had specific, written goals for their future. The answer: 3%. Twenty years later, researchers polled the surviving members of the Class of 1953... and found that *the 3% with written goals had accumulated more personal financial wealth than the other 97% of the class combined!*

It's a coach's and motivational speaker's dream anecdote: a vivid Ivy League success story that documents the cause-and-effect relationship between goals and personal success.

It's convincing! It's compelling! It's also <u>completely untrue</u>!

After an exhaustive search of Yale alumni archives and in-depth investigations into the source of the study (as quoted by Zig Ziglar, Tony Robbins, and others), there is absolutely no evidence that this study EVER took place.

You can't always believe what the gurus say, even if they say it over and over and over again. That's why we depend on science.

USING YOUR BRAIN

Let's look at how your brain handles dreams and goals. When we focus on our dreams, our brain focuses on and imagines our lives as if we have already accomplished them. We focus on what it will be like when, what it will feel like when we are, for example, 20 pounds lighter. As we imagine and focus on this over and over again, our mind actually believes we are 20 pounds lighter (even before we've done anything like alter our diet or exercise). So, when we wake up next week and we aren't any lighter, our brain is confused.

We had clearly set and defined an expectation (a dream or goal) and really concentrated on it in our mind. Then, that expectation wasn't met causing our amygdala (the part of our brain that determines fight, flight or freeze) to become "hijacked." When the amygdala is triggered, we have emotional and physiological responses. We get angry, frustrated, discouraged, disappointed, etc. It's part of the internal processes of our brain. We can do very little to control it once it is triggered. The key is not to trigger it.

Over-focusing on our dreams and goals without actually planning and *doing* anything can really be detrimental to the pursuit of our goals and dreams.

THE NEW APPROACH

Is there a New Approach you should try? Let's take a look at these two questions...

- Who are you trying to become?
- What are you trying to achieve?

These are questions about <u>purpose and accomplishment</u>. Through the years we've found that if you concentrate on purpose, your aim and direction in life, the details take care of themselves.

Most people concentrate on the details. They have endless "to do" lists. You may have lists on your refrigerator, in your Day Timer, in your PDA, on your desk, sticky notes here and there regarding everything you need to do every day of the week for the next year. Is that helping you on your quest of who you want to become? Or is it simply about meeting your deadlines, commitments and standards set by others about what you should be doing?

When we become too goal-oriented, we become almost mechanical in our approach. Our brain loves to conserve energy and form habits. As we keep focusing on solving our problem and reaching our goal, our brain methodically goes through the process and the details. Sounds like that would be good, right? Well, that depends.

A Harvard study (that actually did occur) found that too much goal orientation taught students to solve problems rather than identify opportunities. *The real progress in your life comes from identifying opportunities and choosing to go in the direction of opportunity.* Problem-solving (systemic and extrinsic) is important, but it is just a way to take advantage of opportunities (extrinsic and intrinsic).

Choosing a goal in life is not our most important task or decision. *Choosing the direction is far more important than choosing the goal.* Enticing short-range goals can take us in the wrong direction. True success and satisfaction is in the direction we move, not the goals we attain.

USING GOALS

I want to encourage you *NOT* to set an ultimate goal for your life or even for this year (in the sense of a clear, defined measurable target that you hope to attain). That puts far too much importance on one decision. It can also create futility in those who reach what they initially deemed to be success only to find that it isn't all they dreamed it would be. Think of those who climb to the top of the ladder (success) only to find that it was leaning against the wrong building.

Goals are important to confirm that we are traveling in the direction we intend to go. *Choose your direction, set your sails, and then focus on the process of getting there.* Your goals shouldn't be your destinations, but should instead be a compilation of the steps needed for you to continue in the right direction *TODAY*.

For example, you may say that your goal is to lose 20 pounds. Well, why do you want to lose 20 pounds? I'm pretty sure it isn't because changing your current habits is easy and you just now decided that you'd like to eat healthier and possibly exercise.

So, tell me, why do you want to do it? Is losing 20 pounds in line with who you want to become or what you are trying to achieve in this life? If you are doing it to "feel better" or "get healthier" these are systemic in nature (mental constructs that we create in our minds) you probably won't succeed. If this goal is *NOT* in line with the *intrinsic values* that you hold, the infinite value that you see in your life, you probably won't do it.

However, if you want to lose 20 pounds so that you'll live to see your children get married, or enjoy your retirement with your partner and friends, or some other reason that is far greater than a number on the scale (extrinsic) or idea of how you'll feel (systemic)... well then, you have a chance. Increase your chances of achieving your goal by making sure it is in the direction that you are traveling and a part of the path to becoming who you were intrinsically created to become.

Choosing the direction is far more important than choosing the goal. Here are a few tips to help you on your journey...

- **Choose your DIRECTION**. You don't have to be perfect. The direction just has to be inspiring (focus on the intrinsic nature of your direction). Remember, satisfaction and success come in the direction we move, not in the goals that we attain. Find joy in your journey!

- **Seek Wisdom & Principles**. Identify the principles that you need to continue your journey in your direction of choice. Don't simply follow the tips and techniques of those who've gone before you. Techniques are comparable to fashion - a technique that proved workable yesterday will be unworkable and impractical today. Seek to acquire timeless wisdom!

- **Focus on Improving YOUR SELF**. You are the only you... unique, irreplaceable and invaluable. No one else can ever be you. No one can be you for you. You have to be you yourself. Don't focus on your circumstances. Focus on becoming the best YOU that you can possibly become and enjoy your journey of becoming.

- **ACT, MOVE, GET GOING**! You can't steer a parked car. Don't be paralyzed by fear. You won't fail as long as you keep moving and assessing your direction. Even if you get a little off track, you can correct it as long as you don't stop there. Take a few steps forward, look around and make sure you're headed in the right direction. If not, turn and go forward again. Rinse (act) and repeat.

Once you know *WHO* you want to become and *WHAT* you are trying to achieve, your goals will form the path in your life's direction. Your goals should be the little things that you have to do today - that you have total control over - that keep you pointed in the direction you'd like to go. If a goal isn't along your path, then throw it out. With every goal you set, ask yourself one intrinsically valuable question: *Will this goal keep me headed in the direction of my success?* If the answer is yes, then go for it! (And, OK, now you can write it down.)

Smarter S.M.A.R.T. Goals!

So many people have given up on goal setting. It doesn't seem to work for them. Even "goal-oriented" people are often frustrated by their goals. But for years, the gurus have told you things like:

- "Set S.M.A.R.T. goals (specific, measurable, attainable, realistic and timely). It's a sure-fire way to achieve them."
- "Put pictures of your dream house, your dream car, your dream job all over your bathroom mirror and places where you'll see them every day."

Here's the problem with some of these techniques... they have created an epidemic of people who are unfulfilled, frustrated and dissatisfied with their own performance and success. Goals are supposed to motivate and inspire you, not make you feel like a hopeless, helpless failure.

You are Brilliant! (Yes, I'm talking to YOU)

I'm reading a great book called *Aspire! Discovering Your Purpose through the Power of Words* by Kevin Hall. I recommend it to everyone reading this. In this book, it talks about the word "genius." Did you know that you were a genius? *YOU ARE!!* The word genius comes from the Latin word "genuinus" which means what you were naturally born with. The original word meant "guardian deity or spirit which watches over each person from birth; spirit, incarnation, wit, talent." Genius is nothing more than being true to *YOU*. It's about being genuine and true to your natural talents. It's about unleashing your brilliance.

Why the Frustration?

But, when we set goals, we usually do it backwards. (No wonder it's frustrating!) The vast majority of the gurus assume there is no real difference between skills (which can be acquired) and talents or natural strengths (which you are gifted with at birth). Many gurus think that *natural talents* can be developed through learning, training, and discipline. They fail to appreciate and acknowledge what neuroscience tells us - YOU are born with fixed, deeply-engrained neural pathways and networks that control some of your natural talents. When you fail to see the difference between natural talents and learned skills, you make the bad assumption that both can be equally acquired.

Let's look at how most people set their goals. First, they typically look at the roles that they play, most specifically their jobs. They then identify the talents and skills that they need for a given role and then start trying to develop them. When they do this, they are usually only partially successful. By assuming that training and development will develop natural talents and abilities, many people fail.

In this approach, it appears as though the role is fixed and it is YOU that is broken. Why is it that we revere the job and revile the person? Why is it that the job responsibilities and duties remain fixed and the human being has to change to better fit the job? Does that seem backwards to you? This mindset has caused many people to believe "If there's something that isn't right, it's me that has to change."

YOU DON'T NEED TO CHANGE, YOU JUST NEED REALIGNMENT.

By focusing on the things that you need to change to fit into your job role, you neglect your natural talents. You see, you do not become a genius by trying to be a genius. You become a genius by finding the genius (your natural abilities) that already exists within you and allowing it to be unleashed. *You become a genius by becoming more AUTHENTIC.*

Ralph Waldo Emerson once said, "To be yourself in a world that is constantly trying to make you something else is the greatest accomplishment."

Align yourself and your direction with your strengths!! Fine-tune your goals to be aligned with *WHO YOU ARE!*

As Dr. Seuss says, "You have brains in your head. You have feet in your shoes. You can steer yourself any direction you choose."

Choose to go in the direction of your strengths!

STEPS TO ACHIEVING YOUR GOALS

1) **Decide to be in charge of your life.** I know that may sound kind of silly, but authentic people tend to have a greater belief that they have control over their life and destiny. You can make a difference in how your life turns out.

2) **Uncover your natural strengths**. Try my free assessment (please). You'll find information on this assessment in the Reference section at the end of the book. You results will show you your most balanced thinking habit, your natural neural pathways that make you unique. Then, schedule a free consultation so that we can explore how best to use your natural strength.

3) **Change your thinking about change**. James Allen wrote, "*...we are held prisoner only by ourselves; our own thoughts and actions are the jailors of our fate...*" Don't focus on changing the things that you are not naturally talented in. Focus on finding ways to improve and better utilize your natural strengths. Focus on uncovering and unleashing your natural thinking and valuing habits.

4) **Set goals that you completely control**. Dream big dreams and then look at *WHO* you need to become so that those dreams are rightfully and justly yours. Don't set a goal to get a promotion - you don't control that! Set a goal to acquire the attributes and characteristics of one who would rightfully and justly deserve that position. You can control whether you develop the attributes of

courage, integrity, decisiveness. You can do something every day to improve *YOU!* These are the types of goals that motivate and inspire.

5) **Focus on releasing YOUR BRILLIANCE!** What can you do today to be more real, more genuine, and more authentic? Do you need to work on developing the attribute of courage, compassion, or confidence? Here are two important questions to ask yourself (not your boss or place of work):

- Who do I want to become?
- What am I trying to achieve or accomplish?

6) **ACT!** Your goals are worthless and your dreams are impossible without *ACTION.* Your goals should inspire you to take action. If your goals don't inspire you, then the goals might not be aligned with your natural strengths. When you set goals to improve unnatural talents (instead of skills), they feel more like burdens.

You, my friend, possess unique gifts that were bestowed upon you at birth and that you have developed as a result of everything you have experienced in your life. Be honest enough with yourself to let go of those preconceived notions and habits about how the rest of the world thinks you should be and follow your own path to *WHO YOU ARE.* Being true to you will help you to find your passion and be motivated to act, accomplish and achieve your "true (to you)" goals in life. The things that you dream of can be yours once you become the person you were created to be.

EXAMPLE OF GOAL ACHIEVING PROCESS

On the previous pages I wrote about focusing on goal achieving instead of just goal setting. I wrote about how your frustration is often caused by a misalignment of your natural talents and skills to your current job or position. I then explained the goal achieving process. Many people responded to that asking me for more details or maybe an example. So, I've decided to share my personal goal achieving process with you to let you know what has worked for me in the hope that it will inspire you.

#1 DREAM BIG DREAMS

Don't be afraid to dream big dreams. Many folks that I talk to have been beaten down by the path they've taken in life. They lack the self-confidence to even dream big. I recognize this because I've been there. As a kid, I was going to change the world, then somehow, by the time I was 35 years old the world had changed me.

Look at your life and decide what you want financially, spiritually, personally, relationally. What do you want to accomplish? What legacy do you want to leave? What would you like the people you know to say about you at the end of your life?

For me, well, some of my dreams are this:

- Impact the lives of 1 million people (yes, I put my pinky to my mouth when I say that like in the Austin Powers movie)
- Make over 1 million dollars in a year (no matter what I have to pay in taxes)
- Give away over 1 million dollars
- Be on the cover of *Success* magazine
- Be on ESPN in the game (not just at the game)

#2 Determine Who You Want To Become

Instead of chasing end goals like money and fame, which can leave you feeling empty and maybe even broken in the end, focus on becoming the person who would rightfully have the things that you dream about.

As Og Mandino writes, "I am prepared for wisdom and principles which will guide me out of the shadows into the sunlight of wealth, position, and happiness far beyond my most extravagant dreams until even the golden apples in the Garden of Hesperides will seem no more than my just reward."

I want to be on the cover of Success Magazine. It is a tangible way to know that I have reached my first goal. The people on the cover have impacted the lives of millions of people. Recent covers include Anthony Hopkins, Dave Ramsey, Alicia Keys and Dr. Phil. These are the people who have traits and characteristics that I would like to acquire. I study these people so that I will know which attributes I need to reach my goals. Eventually, I will know that I've reached my goal if my mug is on the cover of that (or an equivalent type) magazine.

#3 Identify Desired Traits & Characteristics

Develop a list of characteristics and traits that are important for you to acquire in order to achieve your dreams. What kinds of attributes, disposition, and constitution do I need to develop to become a person that positively impacts the lives of a million people? My list isn't perfect, but it's what I've come up with so far:

- Empathetic
- Compassionate
- Courageous
- Decisive
- Integrous
- Authentic
- Self-Confident

- Self-Forgiving
- Respectful
- Effective
- Joyful
- Inspiring

#4 Set Goals that Inspire You

Now, the goals that I set are **not** the same as my dreams. I've heard it said that "Goals are dreams with a deadline." If you believe that, I hope that I can change your paradigm today. Most dreams that you have are not under your complete control to achieve. I've had clients say that their goal is to get a promotion by the end of the year. Wow... that's a goal that they have very little direct control over achieving, right? The company and people they work for control their achievement of that goal. Sure, they may be able to do things that improve their chances, but the actual achievement of the goal is not up to them. I don't know if you have noticed this or not, but it's really hard to control other people. ;-)

Your goals should be in alignment with your dreams but should be focused on *attaining the attributes* of the person who rightfully deserves the achievement of their dreams.

So, in my example, I look at what I can do on a daily, weekly, and monthly basis to acquire the traits that I listed above. You see, I have complete control over whether I achieve this or not.

#5 Focus on Your Natural Strengths

In the past, most of my goal setting was focused around my weaknesses. Self-esteem wasn't my strong suit yet if you check out all the books on my shelves, you will find that they are all about self-improvement, self-confidence, and self-love.

Please believe me when I say fixing a weakness is *MUCH* harder than using your natural strengths and strengthening what you are already good at and like to do. Figure out where your strengths lie. We can help you with that and improve your strengths to achieve your goals and dreams!

For me, being empathic and intuitive are my natural strengths even if my low self-esteem caused me to be filled with apprehension and self-doubt. In order to be successful at achieving my goals and fulfilling my dreams, I had to learn to focus on my empathy and compassion which to be quite honest, was fun! It's amazing how people *LIKE* to do the things that they are *NATURALLY* good at doing.

#6 MAP OUT YOUR STEPS

Now, when you look at the list of traits and characteristics that you created in section #3, what ideas come to mind on how to acquire more of these traits? For me, the question is how can a person become more courageous or more decisive? The answer is… the same way we become better at anything in life… *PRACTICE*, more specifically, *deliberate* practice.

The steps to achieving my dream of helping one million people starts with acquiring these attributes. So, I look for activities that I can do on a regular basis that help me to do this. In my case, I chose to umpire Little League Baseball.

Every time I take the field I get to practice *courage*. Have you ever been to a game? The parents and coaches can be brutal! Every game I umpire I get to practice *decisiveness*. I have a split second to decide whether it's a ball or strike, out or safe. I also practice *integrity*. (There are players out there who will tell you that I've told them I messed up a call. It's amazing because they usually say "That's OK.") I also get to practice *self-confidence* and when I do mess up, I get to practice *self-forgiveness*. In my role as umpire, I also try to develop the characteristic of *inspiring others*. I'm told I inspire folks just because I have the guts to be the only female on the field. I try to inspire the coaches and players to be better (even if I occasionally have to eject them from the game). When the parents and spectators misbehave, I get to practice being *empathetic* and *respectful.*

What activities can you do or are you already doing that will/can help you develop the traits that you need to earn your dreams? Do you need to develop consistency as one of your traits? If so, what is it that you can practice doing consistently? Maybe it's making your bed or doing the dishes. I know, it doesn't sound like much but your brain will be developing the neuropathways needed to support you being more consistent.

#7 CELEBRATE YOUR SUCCESS

When was the last time you danced? When was the last time you threw your arms in the air and jumped up and down... for *YOU*?!

You are amazing! You have the ability to transform your life and the lives of others. Celebrate your uniqueness and your successes.

You will probably laugh at me, but I will share a recent example with you. I ordered a foam mattress pad for my bed and it wasn't the right one. Do you know how those things are packaged? They are smooshed and smashed by a machine and rolled into this airtight cellophane wrap. When you unpack it, it expands like those Chinese noodles. Once I realized it was the wrong one, I also realized I had to try to re-roll it and get it back in the box. Well, I can honestly say *"I DID IT!!"* Not only did I do it, but when I was done, I jumped up and down with my arms raised in victory and even hooted a little bit to celebrate my success at achieving what I thought was impossible. Silly? Maybe. But incredibly fun and joyful. Oh, look at that, I got to practice another trait—being joyful!

Take some time today to celebrate your little successes.

FINAL THOUGHTS FOR YOU

I hope that my personal approach has helped you in some way. I also hope that you will apply it to your life. Our clients learn these principles through coaching and it is so amazing to watch what they achieve.

- When you dream big dreams and take the time to focus on *WHO* you want to become in order to achieve those dreams, life is more joyful.
- When you focus on acquiring attributes, you are focusing on acquiring something that can *NEVER* be taken away from you.
- When you set goals that are completely within your power to achieve, you empower your mind, your body and your soul to achieve them.
- When you focus on your God-given strengths, you wake up every morning excited because you want to, get to and choose to be the master of your destiny.
- When you learn to celebrate even the tiniest of your successes, you encourage and inspire yourself to achieve more.

What's truly amazing is that in the process of becoming the person that impacts the lives of one million people, I am also achieving my dream of getting on ESPN. I have been privileged enough to umpire not only for my local Little League but also at the District, Sectional and Texas East State Little League tournaments. Hopefully, in a few years, you'll see me on TV umpiring at the Little League Southwest Regionals or even the Little League World Series.

If you've been frustrated in the past or maybe allowed the world to change you, *take charge today and change your world. You can do it!*

Section 3

Talking To Yourself

FEARS AND FEARLESSNESS

Do you recognize the common fears that may be getting in your way every day? Many times we don't because "we've always been that way."

Some of the common fears that often times unknowingly hold us back are:

- Fear of Success
- Fear of Failure
- Fear of Change
- Fear of Loss or Death
- Fear of Self-Awareness or Introspection
- Fear of Being Judged or Embarrassment
- Fear of the Being Controlled/Out of Control
- Fear of Trusting Others or Commitment

Do any of those resonate with you?

Many who meet me can tell that I love people. I believe in people. I know that people make mistakes and my motto is "love them anyway." However, I've always had a fear of meeting new people. Aren't we all taught not to talk to strangers?

In many cases, we have feared something for so long that we don't even recognize that it is actually fear that is holding us back. Here are a few symptoms that can be attributed to fear:

- Procrastination, Laziness
- Absentmindedness
- Anxiety, Stress
- Social Withdrawal, Distrust
- Restlessness or Always Busy, Busy, Busy
- Overanalyzing or Perfectionism
- Inability To Stay in the "Now"
- Frustration, Guilt, Obligation

Do any of those resonate with you?

If so, they may be born out of your fears.

FEARLESSNESS

Fearlessness: quality of mind enabling one to face danger or hardship resolutely; quality of mind or spirit that faces or endures perils or difficulties. It is characterized by firmness and determination, as in temper, spirit, and actions in order to achieve one's purpose.

To be fearless is to face the reality of your situation without underestimating yourself or deluding yourself that you are more powerful than you really are. And then, at the same time, deciding who you want to be, so that you can stand firm for what you believe in most deeply and so that you can accept criticism (because it will come your way). *Fearlessness is the ability to remain "true" to who you really are despite circumstances.*

Perhaps the most famous quote on being fearless was made by Franklin D. Roosevelt in his first Inaugural Address in 1933:

> *"The only thing we have to fear is fear itself - nameless, unreasoning, unjustified, terror which paralyzes needed efforts to convert retreat into advance."*

STEPS TO ACHIEVING YOUR FEARLESSNESS

What's interesting is that most of our fears are simply thought habits that we've obtained and retained over the years. Initially, these habits protected us from something. But, even when we no longer need the protection, we still have the habit.

For example, let's look at my fear of meeting new people (not talking to strangers). I recognized when I was about 24 years old working as an analytical chemist in a laboratory for a pharmaceutical company that this fear was no longer supporting me. (Although at some point in my life, it probably did support me like when I was a toddler.)

I'd love to tell you that once I realized my fear, I just started meeting new people, but that wouldn't be true. Instead, I told myself that there isn't much opportunity to meet new people in my laboratory because I already knew those 3 people, even though there were 2,000 people that worked on my site. We had a company cafeteria and I would always get my food "to go" and eat it at my desk. Again, I told myself that there isn't much opportunity to meet people at my desk.

OK, to me, that logic seemed very 'reasonable'. You, however, may recognize it as a cop-out or 'rationalization' so that I could avoid meeting new people. *Whatever!* Seriously, I did realize my fear and decided to take a new approach. I decided to talk to people I didn't know at work! Innovative as that was I also added a twist. Since my office was on the 5th floor, I decided that I was going to talk to people in elevators - the one place where people usually don't talk to each other. First of all, it increased the challenge. Secondly, if they didn't respond back to me, I could tell myself that people just don't talk to people in elevators. (Maybe there was another fear in there somewhere?)

The result? People weren't that scary any more. Most of the time they'd even said 'Hi' back to me. As I continued to practice, I continued to grow. This once sabotaging thought habit has now been replaced with a new supporting thought habit. As, Og Mandino says in Scroll 1 of *The Greatest Salesman in the World*:

> *"I will form good habits and become their slave. And how will I accomplish this difficult feat? Through these scrolls, it will be done, for each scroll contains a principle which will drive a bad habit from my life and replace it with one which will bring me closer to success. For it is another of nature's laws that only a habit can subdue another habit."*

Now, I meet new people almost daily. I purposely attend networking events and give speeches to organizations so that I can meet, interact and build relationships with 'strangers'.

So, here are the steps you can take *TODAY* to begin to develop *YOUR FEARLESSNESS!*

1) **Recognize and acknowledge your fears**. This starts with self-awareness. Now, many folks are afraid of self-awareness. They are afraid to see their own shortcomings. Somewhere they developed the thought habit that they had to be perfect. If you're one of these people, overcome that fear today! Take my complimentary assessment and discover a bit more about your internal dialogue and your fears. If you're not one of these folks, then you'll love taking the assessment and learning more about yourself. (If you've taken this assessment in the past, *DO IT* again!)

2) **Decide to improve**. Once you are conscious and aware of your weaknesses, don't be afraid of them. Commit to take the steps necessary to improve any areas of weakness as well as strengthen your strengths.

3) **Plan to break free of the fears that hold you back**. Want help in this area? Get a coach or accountability partner to help you. You really can get to the root cause of your procrastination, your need to be right or in control, your frustration, guilt and stress. Usually it lies within your own mind, your own thought habits and internal dialogue.

Do it!! Begin a program that helps you improve, that holds you accountable for your thoughts and actions, that allows and encourages you to stretch grow, to make mistakes and to become the real, authentic, unique, irreplaceable *YOU*.

The Stories We Tell (Part 1)

Have you ever done something that you didn't really mean to do? Have you ever reacted negatively and then later thought "Why did I do that?" Have you ever told yourself that "From now on I'm going to..." and then didn't keep the promise to yourself or others? Have you ever reacted to someone only to later find out you didn't have the whole story and should've responded differently?

Let's use an example that you may have had or at least seen in the past. You're driving along in traffic, keeping a safe distance between you and the car in front of you, when out of nowhere a car zips up beside you and swerves into the "safe distance" space between you and the car in front of you. This causes you to put on your brakes and re-establish your safe distance.

In that moment, what did you do? Did you cuss, call the person an idiot, or worse? Did you honk your horn? Did you now tailgate the 'idiot' to somehow get back at him or her? Did your hand fly up into the air with only 4 of your 5 fingers in a fist?

Your Everyday Boogie Man

What just happened? You may say, "That person was driving like a maniac and cut me off!!! Someone could've been killed!" I have a question... did you react to a truly terrifying and threatening event? Is the above statement really accurate? In most cases, probably not. You sort of thought they might cut you off as you saw them racing up in your rearview or side mirror so you really had plenty of time to slow down. (In some cases, you may have actually tried to speed up so that they wouldn't cut in, right?) So, why all the drama? I can tell you why. Because in this incident as well as many others throughout your day, you are *NOT* reacting to reality; you are reacting to a fairy tale. This fairy tale is a story that your mind quickly (within milliseconds) created to make 'sense' of what it just perceived. You told yourself a story—maybe it was about right and wrong or what should or should not happen. Your reaction wasn't based on a near tragic collision; it was based on a fairy tale... a story.

Your reaction to this story is not unlike my reaction to the boogie man when the lights went out in my bedroom as a little girl. My mind would tell me that he was under my bed or in my closet. Sometimes the story that I told myself made me get all the way under my covers so that I could seal him out. You know, because the boogie man, in my mind, wouldn't be able to lift up my blanket, right?

REAL LOGIC

So what *REALLY* happened in the driving example above? Seriously, ask yourself that question? Is your 'fairy tale' version the *ONLY* version of the story or could there quite possibly be others? Let's see:

- Maybe the other driver's 'safe' distance is different than your definition of 'safe' distance
- Maybe that 'raving lunatic' driver is trying to rush home to a sick or injured family member.
- Maybe the driver was late for a flight or an important meeting (and you probably have never cut anyone off because of that, right?)

There are countless logical reasons as to why someone else doesn't behave the way that *YOU EXPECT* them to behave. One very important logical reason is because *THEY* are not *YOU!* (If they were you, one of you wouldn't be needed.)

SYSTEMIC RESPONSES

You have systemic responses like this *EVERY DAY*—maybe tens, hundreds or even thousands of times per day. Instead of reacting to reality, you quickly tell yourself a story and react to the Boogie Man!

In almost every reaction to your story, you hijack your amygdala. An amygdala hijack is a phrase coined by Daniel Goleman in his book, *Emotional Intelligence*. You see, under a perceived stress or threat, your cognitive mind shuts down because it takes too long to come to a conclusion. Your amygdala (a tiny part of your brain) takes over and almost instantly decides on fight, flight or freeze. The hairs on the back of your neck stand up. Two tiny organs near your kidneys pump adrenaline into your bloodstream. Your brain diverts blood from activities that it deems nonessential to high priority tasks such as hitting or running. Large muscles in your arms, legs and back get more blood and those high level reasoning areas of your brain get less.

Not only can an amygdala hijack produce physical signs, it can also produce emotional ones as well... fear, hurt, anger, etc. Do you recognize these reactions to situations in your life?

REACTING TO REALITY OR FANTASY

What really happens? You may think that you are logical and always react to reality, but that simply isn't the truth. Your reaction comes not from the external situation but from your internal thoughts. It goes something like this:

Experience --> Tell yourself a story --> Feel --> React

It is *YOUR* stories that create your feelings and emotions. It is your story that explains to you what is going on. It is your story that is interpreting the facts for you. It isn't the behavior or actions of others that are causing your emotions or physiological responses at all—it is the 'boogie man', the fairy tale, your mind's theory of their motives that you are responding to. How could your reaction be different if you didn't make these assumptions as to their intent and their motives? What if you didn't try to 'figure it all out'? Do you *REALLY* know the intent behind their actions? (I know your black/white, right/wrong, systemic mind just told you "Of course, I know their motives. Didn't you see what they just did?")

Let's break down your stories. It usually goes something like this:

1) Your mind implies the intent behind the actions of another person.

2) You dehumanize them by labeling them and/or calling them a name... idiot, maniac, ill-mannered, stupid, @$$hole, etc. (Sometimes you may even be so creative as to combine these names into a long, drawn-out string of expletives, right?)

3) You take offense based on your mind's creativity—the motives that your mind assigned to the action.

4) You react according to your mind's creative story.

Do you recognize this in your life? "Idiot driver, Stupid waiter, Lazy jerk, Crazy sales clerk"

Take a look at what you've become emotional about today. Look at what has frustrated you, angered you, and caused you to feel stressed. Were you stressed because of what actually happened or your mind's story about what happened?

Did you get a phone call from the boss? Did he complain or criticize your work? What story did you tell yourself? Are you blaming him or you for the criticism?

You see when you have a systemic response, it's one *OR* the other. It's a sucker's choice! It's also *NOT* reality! There are thousands if not millions of other choices out there, but your mind only gives you two... either/or. *WRONG!* Your systemic mind's interpretation of reality isn't the same as reality.

MASTERING YOUR STORIES

OK, so I identified a problem, now what? Well, there is a solution. Become a master story-teller!! *IF* you take control of your stories, they can't control you. Any set of facts has an infinite number of stories. Try the following steps:

1) **Analyze your stories**: Take some time each day to relive some of your negative reactions or experiences, but don't relive them as you. Relive them as an unbiased reporter.

2) **Separate facts from fantasy**: Focus on the actions (not the intent behind them). In our example above, the fact is that someone pulled in front of you into the same lane you were traveling in. You had to touch your brakes slightly. Everyone was OK and no accident occurred. Don't confuse your stories with the facts! Remember, no matter how vividly or strongly your mind creates him, the boogie man isn't real.

3) **Watch for emotion-creating words or statements**:

   - Judgment words: "Scowled" (fact: eyes squinted and lips tightened), "Smirked" (fact: eyes squinted and one corner of mouth turned up). In these instances, "scowl" and "smirk" imply intent and motive to a physical observation. "He's stupid." "She's lazy."

   - Extreme words: "Always", "Never", "Everybody", "No one", "Everything", "Nothing"

   - "Either/Or": These two words limit your choices to only two. In reality, you probably have many, many more than that.

   - Assigning blame: "Not my fault, It's all their fault, I had no other choice," i.e., the world's fault.

4) **Recognize that you have a choice**: You can choose to react to the tired old story that your mind gives you out of habit OR you can take control and choose to create new stories. You can be the boss of your mind. It doesn't have to be the boss of you.

5) **Practice new stories**: Now, in place of your old stories, look for options! Did you assign motive or intent? What other motives are

possibilities? The more you practice this the better you will become at listing a whole host of alternative motives. You'll be using your imagination on possibilities instead of problems. Once your creative mind gets used to this, you'll be using it for good instead of, well, the alternatives. You'll be training your mind to react differently the next time a similar situation occurs.

Use your creative, story-telling mind to craft possibilities not limitations... options not ultimatums... positive responses not negative emotions. *YOU* can do it. *YOU* are at choice during these pivotal moments. Sure, it will take practice, but it is not impossible (note: another extreme word).

THE STORIES WE TELL (PART 2)

In the previous section we talked about the stories that we tell to ourselves in our own minds. In this section, we're going to discuss the stories we tell others. Studies show that people think and learn in stories yet many still try to explain things in logical steps. Do you? Do you try to lead by telling and instructing or storytelling?

Some of you may know that I earned a B.S. degree in Chemistry but many of you don't know why. As a matter of fact, many of you may wonder why anyone would want to major in Chemistry. Well, there's a story behind that.

TEACHING THROUGH STORIES

In high school, I had a science teacher who didn't just talk to us about memorizing the periodic table or ionic bonds and electrons. He used *stories* to teach us the basics of chemistry. For instance, instead of just learning the principles of nuclear fission, our science teacher taught us how nuclear reactors were constructed. He taught us what those big towers were used for and how it was a safe and reliable way to produce energy. He taught us through chemistry how the TV, the refrigerator and many other everyday items worked. (And of course, he let us blow things up in a controlled environment.)

One day, he told us about the electrons from the cathode ray tube and how there was a focusing anode that pulled and directed these electrons into a tight beam. This tight, high-speed beam of electrons flies through the vacuum in the tube and hits the flat screen at the other end of the tube. In order to control where the beam lands steering coils are used to create a magnetic field. If you ever looked inside an old-school TV you'd see two sets of coils, one that controls the horizontal motion of the beam and one the controls the vertical motion. (Do any of you remember turning those wheel-like buttons on your TV to stop your picture from rolling?) By controlling the voltages in the coils, you can position the electron beam at any point on the screen. The beam paints every other line as it moves down the screen -- for example, every odd-numbered line. Then, the next time it moves down the screen it paints the even-numbered lines, alternating back and forth between even-numbered and odd-numbered lines on each pass. The entire screen, in two passes, is painted 30 times every second. (It happens so fast, your eyes and brain can't even tell that it's happening.) The screen is coated with phosphor, which emits visible light when struck by the beam. In a color screen, there are three phosphors arranged as dots or stripes that emit red, green and blue light. (Our science teacher told me to go look real closely at our TV and I would see a whole host of red, green and blue dots.) The electrons falling back to their normal state are what emit the color of light. From those 3 colors (RGB), every color on your TV is created. This story was amazing to me!

The stories made chemistry fun and interesting. I mean, there weren't many 13 year old's who could tell you how a TV, refrigerator and nuclear power plant worked. I didn't care to memorize chemical reactions (boring), but I loved knowing what was happening behind the curtain and being able to explain it. These stories made me WANT to learn Chemistry.

STORIES AND EMOTION

There is new research out that shows our emotions can lead to better decisions than our logic. What the studies seem to indicate is that we use logic to explain or justify the conclusions that we've reached emotionally.

As leaders, you can use this knowledge to increase your influence, yet many times in the corporate world we miss out on this important component. Many corporations use the hierarchical command and control type of leadership. You know, "I'm paying you to do a job so just do it." or I'm the boss here, do as I say." How motivated are you to work when that's the environment?

I have a talk that I have given to various organizations about getting 40% more cooperation and productivity from your team. I show empirical evidence that these methods work and work very well. Many of the attendees can see from my examples and stories that it *WILL* work. Yet, inevitably there are a small handful who can believe that it will work, but not for them. Just last week one of them wrote, "Your talk is very practical yet some of what you said just can't happen in today's work environment." In that message, I see conflicting messages. Do you? If it's practical, it can be done, right? But somehow, there is another story that is telling this person that while it can be done, it can't be done where he is. I bet his company doesn't have an environment where stories are used to lead others. Their employees are probably just showing up and doing their tasks. That company is missing out on the latent reserve that people hold back when they don't understand the story behind what they do.

For instance, let's say your job is to walk around a warehouse with an empty box and take items from other larger boxes to fill your box with a variety. Sounds kind of boring, right? Now, let's get a little deeper into the story and let you know that what you are really doing is taking food items from the bigger boxes and creating a single box of food for a homeless family. Knowing the story adds a little more meaning and may give you a little more motivation to do a good job. Now let's say that I took you to the location where you could meet the families who were receiving these boxes of food. What if you were able to see the tears of gratitude in the eyes of the parents as they reached out with trembling hands to receive your incredible gift? How would you feel now about walking around the warehouse filling boxes?

KNOWING THE STORIES

Can you think of any other examples where knowing the story has made a difference? Here are a few:

Let's look at American politics... many people who are able to participate, don't do so. There are bills in Congress that can impact their lives and they are still complacent. Now look what happens when you add stories... just take the healthcare reform bills. If you look at the bill, it is words on a page like any other bill in the past. But, when you add the stories ("everyone will have healthcare benefits" or "there will be death panels", etc.), you get something much different. You get passion, emotion, and a larger number of people who are motivated and involved.

Or, a plane crashes in the ocean killing all 200+ people on board. Sure, you're sad but then you find out you knew someone on board. It 'feels' a little different because now you have a "story" from your past about that person on board. Let's say that the person is a dear relative... now you have a whole host of stories and the emotions are deeper and stronger, right?

And, let's look at all the pink that is worn during the month of October for Breast Cancer Awareness. The NFL had coaches, announcers, and players wearing pink ribbons, pink hats, pink gloves and pink shoes. The goal post padding was pink with a pink ribbon. Those players who have a personal story about a woman in their life having breast cancer probably wore more pink than those who have not been affected. Why? Those who haven't been affected don't have a story. Those who have been impacted probably have a very compelling story.

KNOWING YOUR STORIES

In the previous section, I wrote: "It is YOUR [internal] stories that create your feelings and emotions. It is your [mind's] story that explains to you what is going on. It is your story that is interpreting the facts for you." Knowing this about you also means that it is true for the people you are leading. It is *THEIR* stories that create their feelings and emotions... that provide them with motivation and enthusiasm and passion.

Effective and successful leaders consistently use stories. Effective leaders don't just tell people what to do; they tell them why they are doing it and how their task is part of the bigger story or picture.

- Stories explain.
- Stories elicit emotions.
- Stories change lives by inspiring, motivating and encouraging others to take action.

MASTERING YOUR STORIES

OK, previously I wrote about mastering your internal stories, the stories that your mind tells you. Here are some steps that you can take to master your external stories and become a truly inspirational and influential leader. Try the following steps:

1) **Look beyond the tasks**: Find the true value behind the actions that you are asking others to take. A list of tasks or steps needed to get from point A to point B isn't very inspiring *UNLESS* you know *WHY* you want to go to point B.

2) **Create a (true) story containing INTRINSIC value**: Extrinsic or measurable value can be motivating... like making x dollars or achieving a specified prize. But, *INTRINSIC* value is infinitely more valuable and motivating than the money or prize. Tell a true story that inspires people to do the tasks that they already perform. Show them how they are impacting the lives of others and bringing infinite value to the world.

3) **Call to action**: Once you have shown them the intrinsic value in what they do, call them to action. Allow them to create their own internal stories regarding the value they are bringing to the world.

Allow them to be self-motivated in doing the things they want to do.

4) **Reiterate regularly**: Follow up regularly with your stories. Update your stories with more information and more value. This will remind your followers that what they are doing is making a difference.

5) **Practice your stories**: Becoming a good storyteller doesn't happen overnight. Be willing to practice telling your stories every day. Search for the intrinsic value and the true meaning behind what you do.

Use your creative, story-telling mind to craft possibilities not limitations... options not ultimatums... positive responses not negative emotions.

YOU can do it. *YOU* are at choice during these pivotal moments. Sure, it will take practice, but it is far from impossible.

THE STORIES THEY TELL US

As I talk with my clients, I am shocked with how many believe and take to heart the things that *others* say *about* them. I know we as humans value other people and their opinions of us. You try to please other people and live up to their beliefs often at your own expense. Are you a *people-pleaser*? Even if you spout off saying "I don't care what anyone else thinks" (like some teenagers do), it's simply human nature to care. And, chances are there is at least one other person whose opinion of you that you care about. That person may be your spouse or your kids... your boss or your peers... your fellow church-goers or your poker buddies. So what stories are they telling you about you?

YOUR BELIEFS CONTROL YOUR DESTINY

The belief you have in yourself determines everything that you do. Yet many times, you didn't come to that belief yourself. The belief that you have in what you can and cannot do, who you can and cannot be, came from others... your teachers, coaches, parents, pastors, bosses, peers, even the bullies from school. These folks have told you stories about you and you unconsciously believed them.

You may have heard the story of the young man who fell asleep in his math class. He woke up as the bell rang, looked up at the blackboard, and copied down the two problems that were written there. He assumed they were the homework for the night. He went home and labored the rest of the afternoon and into the evening knowing if he didn't complete the work he would surely fail the class. He couldn't figure out either one but he kept trying for the rest of the week. Finally, he got the answer to one and brought it to class. The teacher was absolutely stunned. The boy feared he had done too little, too late. It turned out the problem he solved was supposedly unsolvable.

How did he do it? He was able to do what was thought to be impossible because he believed it was possible. He not only believed it was possible, he believed that if he didn't solve it he would fail the class. Had he been told the problem was *unsolvable* he could never have done it.

Have you looked at your beliefs about you lately?

I often ask clients what they believe are their strengths. After they think for 15-45 seconds, sometimes longer, they usually come up with something. I then ask how they know that's their strength. Most of the time I'll hear something like "A lot of people tell me that." or "That's consistent in my performance reviews." This is interesting to me because rarely do they say "I've just always enjoyed doing it and have practiced it for <x> amount of time."

The opposite is also true. When I ask my clients what their greatest challenges are, they are *MUCH* quicker at listing those, of course. But when I ask how they came up with that list, they again say "That's what my boss or spouse or teacher has said about me."

This made me think... *Where do you get your opinions about you?*

Please take some time to think about that. *It's really important* because here's what I discovered. Most of my life I listened to the opinions that others had about me and those opinions became my opinions of me. To be open with you, here were some of the comments: "Traci's pretty smart, but she's not a good speaker." "Traci's a good athlete, but has a bad attitude." "Traci is too emotional - a big baby - and laughs too loud." "Traci is tactless." "If Traci goes to that school and majors in Physical Education, she'll end up being a dumb jock." These were all said to me when I was a kid by adults whom I respected.

For years, no, for decades, those opinions from others were my reality. But the truth is: *the stories that other people tell you about you are NOT facts!!* They are opinions and perspectives. Their opinions and perceptions are based on their *LIMITED* views and understanding. *When you choose to allow their opinions to become your reality, it's YOUR fault.*

STORIES YOU'VE BEEN TOLD

One of my clients has a boss that believes (and tells her) that "You are only as good as your worst mistake." Wow, that's pretty harsh and also sad, but it is the perception of her supervisor. At first, I don't think that she believed this statement, but as it was repeated over and over, she allowed it to control her behaviors, actions and decisions. Normally, she loved trying new things and inspiring change. Now she was afraid of messing up and being characterized and known for her mistakes.

As time passed and she, of course, still had to report to her boss, she would receive negative comments from him. His *stories* about her performance were usually unfavorable. He perceived the world through pessimistic lenses. When my client would go into see her boss I imagined that he did have a few valuable or worthwhile suggestions and comments, but he also had a lot of comments that were worthless to her. I asked her why she left the "$100 bills" in his office and choose to walk out carrying the turds. (Yes, I really said turds to my client.) You see when she heard a comment that had value I imagined it to be a hundred dollar bill and she could choose to receive it from him. Instead, she had been choosing to pick up his negative comments. These were just turds. (Sorry, if that word offends you. But it accurately depicts something that is not only worthless but really stinks - a great analogy in my mind.) Now, who wants to pick up and carry a turd around all day (or all week or all year)?

As we discussed this situation she realized that:

Someone's temporary opinion of you does NOT have to be your permanent reality!!

How often does this happen to you? Are you in the habit of picking up the turds that others set out before you? When you go in to talk to your boss (maybe even your spouse) or receive your performance review, do you hear and pick up the good things that are said? Or, do you simply look at the negative comments and what you're not good at?

Do you realize that you are at the point of CHOICE?

You, and only you, get to determine whether or not someone else's opinion of you becomes your reality!

WRITING YOUR OWN STORIES

As I write this and the winter holiday season is fast approaching. Here in America we will celebrate Thanksgiving. While many of us will take time to be thankful for the things that we have, I'd like to encourage you to *be thankful for the person YOU are*. You are unique, priceless and irreplaceable! You have gifts and talents like no other human being on earth. Try the following steps to help you realize your potential to use your unique gifts and talents:

1) **Question Your Current Beliefs About You**: What worked in the past may not be working now. Take some time to look at your thoughts. Some are supporting your success while others are sabotaging you. Question them! Remember, you are *NOT* your thoughts and they aren't the boss of you (unless *YOU* allow them to be.)

2) **Develop Your Own Opinions and Perspectives**: When you find that you are reiterating a belief that someone else told you, look into it. There are sooooo many rumors and myths that are believed to be true. For instance, where would you think the Battle of Bunker Hill took place? Wrong. It mostly took place on Breed's Hill in the Charleston section of Boston. Colonel Prescott was supposed to establish defensive positions on Bunker Hill according to orders from General Putnam. But Prescott didn't make it there. The resulting conflict was called the Battle of Bunker Hill because that is where Prescott originally intended—

and was ordered—to build the fortifications. Question the "facts" and come to your own conclusions!

3) **Don't Pick up the Turds**: If someone is giving you advice or feedback, analyze each part by asking yourself the question "Does that (or would that) *ADD* value to my life or the lives of others?" It's pretty simple. If the answer is "Yes", pick up the advice. Don't jump to any emotional conclusions; just seek out the value. If you don't find the value, then it's probably something stinky and worthless that you don't want to take with you.

CAUTION: When you don't value the advice, opinion or perspective of another, be sure that you don't *DEVALUE* them as a person. Remember that their perceptions are based on their experiences, many of which you have no knowledge of. Be sure that your mind doesn't tell you "They're stupid." or say "What an idiot!" That also adds no value. Besides, they, like you, are an infinitely valuable, unique, priceless and irreplaceable human being.

4) **Understand, Multiply (and Be Thankful for) Your Strengths**: By questioning other's perspectives and looking for the value, you will be better equipped to understand *YOU*. You will be able to look for the value that *YOU* bring. Once you find that, strengthen that strength. (I help people to do this every day and they are amazed at how quickly they can change something that they've wanted to change for decades when they take this approach.)

Og Mandino writes:

"Today I will multiply my value a hundredfold.
A mulberry leaf touched with the genius of man becomes silk.
A field of clay touched with the genius of man becomes a castle.
A cypress tree touched with the genius of man becomes a shrine.

A cut of sheep's hair touched with the genius of man becomes raiment for a king.
If it is possible for leaves and clay and wood and hair to have their value multiplied a hundred, yea a thousandfold by man, cannot I do the same with the clay which bears my name?"

You see, I am thankful that I learned to choose my own beliefs. There are many other people who are thankful that I did as well. Through my work, I am able to speak to thousands of people every year. I am blessed to have some approach me and say that my words and stories made a positive difference in their life. I'm not saying this to toot my own horn. I'm saying this because someone with "a bad attitude", who "couldn't control her emotions", and who was "a terrible public speaker" shouldn't be able to have this kind of impact. *By choosing not to live the life that others paint for you, you too can multiply your value a hundredfold, yea a thousandfold.*

You can change your life (and maybe even the lives of others) by being selective and being "at choice" when it comes to the stories that THEY tell you. Choose to believe those that add value to your life and leave the turds behind. *Remember: Someone's opinion of you does NOT have to be your reality!!*

Og Mandino concludes Scroll 8 of *The Greatest Salesman in the World* by saying:

"Today I will multiply my value a hundredfold.
"And when it is done I will do it again, and again, and there will be astonishment and wonder at my greatness..."

I can't wait for you to see the greatness that you bring to the world!

Success AND Failure

To continue to help you be a better leader I wanted to focus on your mindset. There are so many myths out there as well as stories and depictions that don't really add value or help you create success in your life or your leadership.

For example, many success gurus purport a 1953 Yale Study that proved that the 3% of graduates who wrote down their goals accounted for 97% of the class' wealth. Have you ever heard of this study? Truth is: It never happened.

How about the story that your mom told you: if you swallow your gum it will take 7 years to digest? Nope. That's not true either. (And if you ever swallowed any of that fluorescent Gator Gum, you already knew that.)

The Road to Success

How about this depiction?

It's also a myth!

It looks like the road to success goes in one direction and the road to failure goes in the opposite direction. This can create what we call the "sucker's choice." Either you have to choose success OR you have to choose failure. The sucker's choice is rarely the correct perspective.

It's another one of those myths which won't add value to your life. It is simply not the truth and will probably take away value from your life. If you continue to believe this *IS* the road sign of life, you can unintentionally create a sabotaging mental habit or mindset that keeps you from your success, your goals, and your dreams.

The road to success is paved with failures. Failure is the price that you pay for your success. If you spend your time trying to avoid failure, you will get what you pay for. You will probably be standing still or going in the same vicious circle you've been going in for years.

The course you take to success *WILL* have failure stops along the way. The real question for you is: how effectively do you manage those failures?

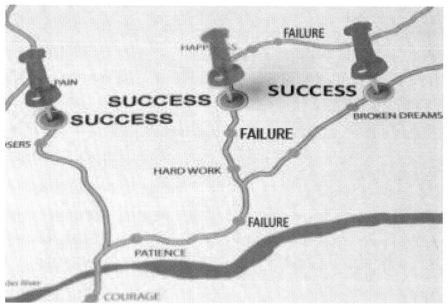

Also, you'll notice in the picture above that there isn't just one road that leads to your success. I believe that even if you make a wrong turn you can still get there, it just may take a little longer, but you can still enjoy exploring the new areas on your journey.

YOUR MENTAL PROGRAMS

Our minds have been programmed to believe that failure is the final step. Remember in school, if you failed your test, you failed. Might as well paint the big loser *L* on your forehead. Oh, and remember those kids that were "held back." They were branded failures for years. Really? They were failures? *NO!* Of course not. But as we go through life, we see examples of this everywhere.

Lose and you must be a loser. Fail and you must be a failure. Leaders who see failure as the opposite of success aren't leaders at all; they are critics, judges and autocrats. This mindset in a leader is very dangerous for those whom they lead. A leader who believes failure is not part of success will have a team that is slow moving if moving at all. Team members will be idling in park afraid of moving forward. If they are idling in park, do they really need a leader? I mean, you can't steer a parked car, can you?

What's amazing is that in America (and probably elsewhere around the world), we love to see the great comeback! You know, that someone who really messes up and then overcomes their failures or shortcomings. Do you realize that you would never see a comeback if people avoided failure or never failed? There would be no second chance for Michael Vick or Tiger Woods... no second chance for Ben Affleck, Elton John or Drew Barrymore after their drug addictions. (Yet there are some with the "fail and you are a failure" mindset that don't care to see them make it.) Every President of the US would be a failure. Every CEO, teacher, lawyer, doctor, garbage collector... OK, every human being would be a failure with this closed mindset.

Success is not an "either/or" scenario. (We call that systemic in the world of axiology.) Success is rarely systemic. The real secret of success is that there is no secret!! It's an "either/and/and" scenario. You can fail *AND* succeed. You will become a success *AND* fail. The difference between success and failure simply lies in your response to the inevitable failures you encounter along the road of life.

How do you respond to these "inevitable failures"?

- Do you avoid them at all costs?
- Does your mind tell you that if you fail you are a failure?
- Are you so focused on perfection that you are sometimes paralyzed from taking a chance?
- Do you spend hours/days/months beating yourself up when you make them?
- Do you escape and imagine what life will be like when you are a success?

These choices can all be dangerous and derail you from your path to success.

YOU CAN CHOOSE TO THINK DIFFERENTLY.

You can choose to look for challenges even if you may fall short.

You don't get stronger by looking at the weights; you get stronger by picking them up. You get stronger through the challenge. Leaders don't fear the resistance, they embrace it. It's the "getting back up" despite how far or how hard you have fallen that builds your strength and leadership.

- Leaders help others to learn! They don't just tell them what to do.
- Leaders allow others to think and grow in the direction of *THEIR* talents to achieve *THEIR* success.
- Leaders help others to prepare for failures and give them tools for reaching their success.
- Leaders help others to overcome their failures. They don't point fingers and blame.
- Leaders are not afraid to be the example of overcoming failure on their road to success!

I wish you many challenges and failures because I am certain they will lead to your great success, joy and happiness!!

Section 4

Beginning Your Growth

DEVELOPING A MOTIVATED MINDSET

Our society worships talent—just look at how much we pay our athletes and star performers. Many people assume that possessing superior skill or intelligence—along with confidence—is the recipe for success.

However, Carol Dweck, a Psychology professor at Stanford University, says that more than 30 years of scientific investigation suggests that an overemphasis on intellect or talent leaves people a) vulnerable to failure, b) fearful of challenges and c) unwilling to remedy their deficiencies.

Can you believe that? How can over-focus on brain power and talent prevent us from succeeding? Those seem a bit counter-intuitive but let's look at this in more detail through the theory of "mindsets".

THEORY OF MINDSETS

One theory says that there are two general classes of learners: fixed mind-set and growth mind-set.

People who have a **fixed mindset** believe that "they are the way they are." They believe that intelligence, skills, and leadership are fixed traits. That doesn't mean that they have less of a desire for a positive self-image than anyone else. They do, of course, want to look good, smell good and perform well. Yet, there are some characteristics evident in those with a fixed mindset:

- They Avoid Challenges—Rather than risk failing and negatively impacting their self-image, they will often avoid challenges and stick to what they know they can do well.
- They Avoid Obstacles—They would rather give up easily than risk not overcoming.
- They Ignore Negative Feedback—Well, ignore is the best of cases; feedback is often taken as an insult. They believe that

any criticism of their capabilities is criticism of them personally.

- <u>They are Threatened by the Success of Others</u>—They will try to convince themselves and the people around them that the success of others was due to either luck or unethical actions.
- <u>They Believe Effort Is Fruitless</u>—Hard work doesn't pay because "you are what you are", "you can only do what you can do".

Do you know of anyone like that? Do you, at times, feel like that?

Let's now look at a **growth mindset**. People who hold the growth mindset believe that intelligence is malleable and can be developed through education and hard work. Characteristics of those with a growth mind-set are:

- <u>Motivated by Challenges</u>—You embrace challenges because you know you'll come out stronger on the other side.
- <u>Persist in the face of Setbacks</u>—Obstacles or external setbacks do not discourage you. Your self-image is not tied to your success or how you will look to others. Failure is an opportunity to learn, so whatever happens you win.
- <u>Effort is Necessary</u>—Effort is needed for you to grow and learn and master your skills.
- <u>Feedback is a Source of Information</u>—That doesn't mean that all criticism is worth integrating or that nothing is ever taken personally, but at least you know you can change and improve.
- <u>Inspired by the Success of Others</u>—Success is a source of inspiration and information. Someone doesn't have to fail for you to succeed. There aren't a fixed number of successes in the world. Success is not a zero-sum game.

THE CONCLUSION

Which mindset do you typically identify with? Does it depend on your surrounding circumstances?

More importantly... *can you change your mind-set?*

If you are someone or know of someone who has a fixed mindset, what can you do about it? If you have children, what can you do to ensure that they develop a healthy, growth mind-set?

How many times have you said, "You're so smart," or "Wow? You're gifted." OK, maybe not recently to your peers and co-workers, but have you ever said it to children. I know I have... but I won't be doing that any more. Here's why...

According to the research, 85% of parents believe that praising children's ability or intelligence when they perform well is important for making them feel smart. Studies, however, showed that praising a child's intelligence make them feel fragile and defensive. Did you catch that? *Praising intelligence or a "gift" of talent can actually make the person feel fragile and defensive.*

You see, Dr. Dweck found that praising traits that children may not think they have much control over can actually demotivate them. When you say to a child, "You are so cute," there's not much that they can do with that. Either the cuteness gods have blessed them or not. Praising cuteness can actually make the child feel insecure if they ever don't feel cute or don't feel special when someone doesn't think they are cute.

Now, if you compliment a child by saying "It looks like you really worked hard on that project." Now they are being praised for their hard work, which they do have control over in the future. You can motivate them to continue to put forth the effort to achieve their goals.

In our coaching practice, we often tell our clients to focus on the process, not the outcome. (The outcome is important—don't get me wrong. But if you're not enjoying the journey, chances are the outcome will fall short of your expectations.) Likewise, to encourage those around you to have a growth mind-set, *praise the process*. *Praise the effort* involved in taking the steps toward progress and success. *Praise hard work and dedication*. That, my friend, is what encourages a growth mindset in those around you.

THE APPLICATION

It is vitally important that we correct our fixed mindset and help others to do the same. In the work environment, you can recognize those with a fixed mind-set because these folks are:

- Less willing to admit their errors
- Less willing to confront their deficiencies in their work or relationships
- More likely to ignore constructive criticism or advice from others
- Less likely to seek feedback or welcome input and ideas
- Less likely to mentor or coach their underlings

Individuals with a growth mindset are people who believe that people can change and grow. This is the type of person I strive to help you become. So, how can I do that?

GROWING YOUR MIND-SET

What can you do *TODAY* to improve your mindset and the mindset of others? Try these steps:

1) **Understand that your brain is like a muscle**. Learning really does prompt neurons in the brain to grow and create new connections. This process is never-ending. It is a dangerous and hurtful myth that you are born with a set number of brain cells.

2) **Focus on the process instead of the outcome**. Our brain can get so set and focused on the outcome that the steps necessary to get there produce feelings of frustration and discouragement.

3) **Praise the process**. Use statements like: "That was difficult, but you stuck with it and got it done." "Mistakes are learning experiences. Let's see what we can learn from this one." "I'm impressed with how you worked through that difficult situation. You are going to learn a lot of great things." If these statements don't come naturally, practice them daily.

4) Realize that **hard work and discipline** contribute much more to achievement than IQ does. Even what we call genius or talent is typically the results of years of dedication and passion, not something that flows naturally from a gift.

If we foster a growth mindset in our businesses, careers, homes and schools, we will give those around us the tools necessary to succeed in their pursuits and become personally accountable for their own success. That's a wonderful intrinsic gift to give to those around you!

What's ~~Wrong~~ Right with You?!?

"Fear less, hope more;
Eat less, chew more;
Whine less, breathe more;
Talk less, say more;
Love more, and all good things will be yours."
  - Swedish Proverb

I love that quote above because it has one of my all-time favorite words in it five times. That word is *more*. I love that word because it's never-ending. You can always have and be *more*. More today than yesterday and more tomorrow than today.

So, how does that play into "What's *RIGHT* with You" which is the title of this section? Well, in life, we seem to find more of what we look for. You can seek more joy and find it. Or you can choose the mindset of seeking more pain and find it as well.

WHAT IS YOUR FOCUS?

So many people have been trained most of their lives to look for risks (i.e., what can go wrong). Starting in elementary school, we're taught to solve problems. That's what homework is all about... read this and solve these *problems*.

When are we going to learn that the greatest success comes from *seeking opportunities* not finding and identifying problems and challenges? When are learning institutions going to give their students exercises on finding opportunities?

OPPORTUNITY VS. RISK

Our brains are trained from a young age to look at what's wrong. Our self-worth is sometimes defined by how many problems that we can fix or avoid. Many people think that the brain *naturally* functions that way. I believe that it has been coached and trained to think that way. Sure, the brain has a natural instinct for recognizing errors, but the mind can choose what to focus on.

From entrepreneurs to project managers to sales people... you are taught to find the pain, the problem... to look for what's wrong and come up with a solution. It sounds logical and it is helpful (please don't misunderstand my point.)

Let's look at the people that have "made it", who are highly successful and wealthy. Since I have an Information Technology background, let's look at Steve Jobs and Bill Gates. These are two highly successful gentlemen. They have changed the lives of millions and millions of people.

Did they do it by looking for problems?

Or, did they do it by looking for opportunities?

I believe, more than solving problems, they sought out opportunities. They looked for what was "right" and added "more." Bill Gates didn't invent the computer. He did, however, see an opportunity to make it "personal." Steve Jobs didn't invent music, but he found an opportunity to make it convenient.

Do you own an iPod or iPhone? Why? Why did you buy it? Were you in pain? Did you have a problem listening to your CDs or the radio?

No. These men became wealthy because they *CREATED* the market. They didn't "fix" anything that was wrong. You didn't even know you needed an iPod until Apple created it. They saw an opportunity!

LOOK FOR WHAT'S RIGHT

I want to encourage you to *LOOK* for what's *RIGHT* and build instead of looking for what's wrong and correcting or destroying it.

Let's look at a few examples:

Youth Sports: As you may know, I umpire Little League baseball and I competed in competitive sports from grade school through college. I am amazed at how parents and grandparents will cheer *AGAINST* the other team and officials. They are so focused on what's wrong that they forget about what's right! They teach their kids to focus on what's wrong... creating victims of "bad" calls and "unfair" play instead of creating victors who overcome, learn and grow. They are giving the participants an excuse to fail... instead of encouraging them to try harder and smarter to achieve more.

<u>Managers</u>: I spent many years as a manager in the corporate world and had to do those performance evaluations. What did the evaluations focus on? You got it! We told you what was wrong with you and what you needed to 'fix' so that you could better fill your role. What would happen at your company if they looked at the strengths of their employees and asked them to get stronger at what they are already good at? What if they looked for roles that you could fill by using more of your strengths? Employees would actually like going to work and contribute more.

LOOK FOR WHAT'S RIGHT WITH YOU

My focus today isn't so much about fixing what's wrong with youth sports or management as demonstrated in the examples above. As usual, my focus is on you.

Often I ask my clients and audiences, "When was the last time you celebrated you?" Have you taken the time to celebrate your natural strengths and the things that you do right? I've heard others complain "No one even noticed my contribution." So what? If you are waiting for someone else to celebrate your contribution, you aren't looking for what's *RIGHT* with you (you're waiting for someone else to do it for you).

YOU DECIDE! Choose today to look for what's right with you. Celebrate your goodness and your strengths. Celebrate *WHO YOU ARE* as well as what you do and accomplish. Learn to look for opportunities to use your natural, God-given strengths and you will start to see the world from a new perspective.

Choose to ask others "What's right with you?" instead of focusing on what's wrong with them. Help others to see opportunities for growth... opportunities to add value... opportunities for "more."

MAKE A LIST

I want you to take a few minutes to make a list of the things that are right with you... maybe even the things you can celebrate. Yes... I mean right now. It'll only take a couple of minutes. I'll even help you to start it.

1) **"I am priceless."** There is no one else in the world like you. You have a combination of talents and gifts that are unique in this world.

2) **"I am intelligent."** You *HAVE* to be intelligent if you're still reading this book. ;-)

3) **"I am loved."** If no one else loves you (which I highly doubt), I do! Yes, and I might not know you that well, but I do know that you are a good human being with a desire to make a positive difference and I love you for that.

4) _____.

5) _____.

6) _____.

Seriously, don't just skip over those blank lines. Take a minute to write down what you think is *RIGHT* with you! I'll wait...

What if you're stuck and can't think of anything to celebrate or anything that is *RIGHT* with you? Let me help!!

IMPROVING YOUR REALITY

Your brain creates your reality. How much time do you spend thinking about your brain? Do you ever pay attention to your brain? Today we're going to discuss your brain's role in perception and reality. We'll also see if you have A.N.T.s in your brain.

John Milton in *Paradise Lost* wrote, "The mind is its own place, and in itself can make a heaven of hell, a hell of heaven."

In life, it is not what happens to you that determines what you do or how you feel; it is how your mind perceives reality that makes it so. So, how has your mind been making your reality?

Most people are unaware of how their thinking clouds their reality. They are unaware that they are not controlled by events or other people but by the perceptions their brains make of those events and people.

Take the stock markets across the world. Some people are saddened, depressed and even angry over the falling stock prices. They see the value of their portfolios or 401k accounts dropping by 40% and react to their perception that the stock market is too risky so they pull their funds out of the market and put it in *safer* investments (or under their mattress). Compare that to the people who saw the same drop of 40% in their investments and are excited. They are looking for cash to BUY more stocks because they view the current situation as a SALE... everything is 40% off!!

What's the difference? *Reality* is still reality. The stock market is down. But, their brains see the same situation from different perspectives and they will obtain different results. Understand that the view your brain takes of a situation, event or person has more reality in it than the actual situation itself.

REALITY AND PERCEPTION

Your perceptions bear witness to your state of mind and the state of your brain. *What you see in life is based on your INNER view of the world formed by the neural connections of your mind.* As your brain functions, so you perceive.

Dr. Daniel Amen in his book, *Making a Good Brain Great*, talks about a formula that he writes out for his patients:

$$A + B = C$$

A = Actual Event

B = Brain's interpretation or perception of the event

C = Conclusion or how you react to the event

Most people think that (**A**) the things that happen to you determine your (**C**) behavior. Actually, it is the **B** part (your brain's interpretation or perception of the event) that largely determines how you respond. You spend a lot of your time, energy and money trying to change **A** thinking that it will change **C**. Other people and events (**A**) cannot make you do anything. It is your brain's interpretation or perception (**B**) that causes your behavior (**C**).

You should seek not only to change your outside world by learning different tips and techniques to manipulate and influence, but also (and more importantly) seek to change your inside world or how your brain perceives situations.

Here's a key point: *Just as your brain can distort reality, it can also improve it!!*

IMPROVING YOUR REALITY

Here are three steps to improving your reality (as taken, in part, from Dr. Amen's book referenced above):

1) <u>Do not believe every first thought that your brain gives you.</u> It is incredibly easy to misunderstand or misinterpret a situation. How

many times have you read an email and come to a conclusion only to find out your assumption wasn't what the other person meant. Every day I work with clients who are learning which thoughts are most likely to distort their reality. The VQ Profile measures your thought processes. Your results can pinpoint areas your life that occur throughout your day where you are most likely to incorrectly perceive reality.

2) <u>Realize that your thoughts are extraordinarily powerful...</u>

...Especially your systemic thoughts that can also trigger emotional and physiological responses. When you look at your 6 Advisors assessment, click on the Systems Thinking and Self-Direction tabs, do you see bars that are yellow, orange or even red? If so, there is a good chance that you will not only THINK these thoughts but you will also FEEL them. You will feel as though your reality (based on your perceptions) is the only reality. If others respond differently than you, it is because they are not seeing things straight. You will actually feel emotional and physiological responses within you—like when someone cuts you off in traffic or doesn't meet your expectations. The emotions and physiological responses associated with these thoughts often make them extraordinarily powerful.

3) <u>Recognize that thoughts lie, are easily distorted, and can rob you of joy.</u>

Many people's brains are filled with A.N.T.s. OK, not the little bug kind of ants, but Automatic Negative Thoughts. These A.N.T.s can come in different shapes and sizes (just like the real ants). Let's look at some of the different species of ants and how they relate to your Automatic Negative Thoughts.

   a. **Picnic ANTs**... These are just the little annoying ones that invade a picnic or other happy occasion. They start out small, maybe one or two in number, and then the army invades.

b. **Flying ANTs**... These are always buzzing around and you just never know where they are going to land or show up.

c. **Bulldog ANTs**... These are aggressive, vicious and exhibit powerful bites. Their nests may be inconspicuously hidden under a rock and can surprise you with an attack.

d. **Carpenter ANTs**... These thoughts gnaw and eat at the structure in your 'home' or mind. They nest there and come out to scavenge for other foodstuffs (thoughts) throughout the day.

e. **Fire ANTs**... These start out looking innocuous and then they bite you! Not only does it hurt when they bite you but they leave you with a bite that itches and stings for days.

f. **Bullet ANTs**... Named on account of its powerful and potent sting, which is said to be as painful as being shot with a bullet. (Have you ever been hit with one of these thoughts? Ouch!)

Your Automatic Negative Thoughts (ANTs) can act or behave as each of these types of real ants.

How are your ANTs impacting your life? Your spouse's life? Your career? Your spiritual life? Your financial life? Your children's lives?

Understanding that they are simply thoughts produced by the neural pathways in your brain can help you to become more aware of their impact. That understanding can also give you hope because you can change those neural pathways and habits.

CHANGING YOUR BRAIN

The latest breakthroughs in neuroscience have shown us that what the gurus told us in the past just doesn't work. The *compensation approach* doesn't produce real, lasting changes. You know this approach. It's where your *FOCUS* is on *FIXING* the bad habit. You are told to do things like...

- Think the opposite of an ANT (automatic negative thought)
- When you start to think negative...Think Positive
- Feel the pain and do it anyway
- Fake it till you make it

These approaches just don't work and here's why...

Imagine if you will that you have a bad habit, an ANT. (I know you don't have any, that's why I said 'imagine.' wink-wink). So, let's say that you'd like to lose weight, i.e., you are going to *FIX* your weight problem. Now imagine that you used the compensation approach and when you think about, say, eating something unhealthy like potato chips, you train yourself and practice instead to immediately think about eating an apple.

We know that the brain will then make a neural connection between these two thoughts, eating potato chips and eating an apple. By continuing this practice, you will hardwire these two thoughts together. So, now, if I mention an apple, your brain will think also of potato chips. (Electricity doesn't discriminate and will flow in either direction along the wired connection.)

So, when you have a bad habit and you choose to associate it with a good thought, you've actually started a little battle in your brain along your new neural connection. These two thoughts compete to see which will win to produce your action. (Do you sense this battle going on in your mind?)

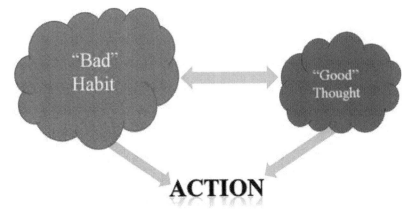

ACTION

This compensation approach takes a LOT of energy and discipline to make real, lasting changes. Yet, in stressful situations, where your brain doesn't have a lot of extra energy, your brain will choose the path of least resistance... which is your old bad habit. Have you noticed this pattern in your life?

SO, WHAT DOES WORK? <u>THE NEURO-AXIOLOGICAL APPROACH</u>!

Now, imagine that you still have that bad habit of eating potato chips. Separate from that thought, you identify a change that you would like to make in your life like eating more apples. This new good thought must have real value to you (for instance, eating apples will make you healthier and your health is valuable to you).

If that thought is also based in *your natural strength* (a balanced thought process) like valuing your physical health or valuing the ones you love and living a long life for them, you can naturally rely on the good thought to produce a good action. You see, it isn't connected with a bad habit like eating unhealthy food or trying to diet. In and of itself this good thought has real value and is based in a natural thinking strength of yours where there is no need for a connection (hardwiring) to the bad habit. *The FOCUS is not on changing a bad habit but solely on creating a new one.*

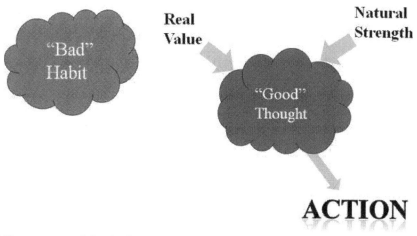

The neuro-axiological approach allows you to...

- Consciously choose to focus to a more useful, *good*, thought process.
- See the real and independent value in creating a good thought habit.
- Anchor your thinking in a natural, strong thought process.

As your brain continues to use this good thought, the bad thought which is no longer being triggered or exercised, will 'atrophy'. In neuroscience, they call it *synaptic pruning*...what your brain doesn't need or doesn't use, it prunes away.

In order to change your behavior and change your reality, you MUST stop focusing on CHANGE and start focusing on VALUE!

To change your brain, you must focus on your natural strengths and the real value in the good thought!

CONSIDER THESE THINGS....

- Do you know your natural strengths?
- Can you recognize the thoughts that are causing your mind to distort reality?
- Would you like to find out?
- Improving your reality is up to *YOU!*

- Will you choose to take control of your *INNER* life (B) and effectively change your outcomes (C)?
- Or, will you continue to allow your bad thinking habits, your ANTs, determine your reality?

The choice is yours, every single day.

LESSONS FROM THE LOSER'S BRACKET

At the end of July 2009, I had the honor of umpiring the 10 year-old bracket of the Texas East State Little League Championships. I know, you may be thinking (as did one of the 10 year-old participants), "I never saw a girl umpire before." But it's really true. I have pictures to prove it.

One of the good things about umpiring is that you learn something new every game. I wanted to share some of the wisdom that I learned from the coaches and managers in the loser's bracket of the tournament. Now, this isn't going to be just about baseball, but the wisdom and lessons that can be applied to your leadership skills.

But first let me explain the "loser's bracket." At Texas East State, the tournament is run as a double elimination between four sectional champions... that means that you have to lose twice before you are eliminated and have to go home. If your team happens to lose one game, you are placed in what is called the "loser's bracket" until you lose a second time. Got it?

One of the unique aspects of being an umpire is that you always have one of the best seats in the house for observing the game. I take advantage of this opportunity to see how the coaches coach and lead their teams. Below are just a few of the "words of wisdom" that I heard from the managers at the Texas East State Championship in 2009.

"DON'T SWING AT NOTHIN' UGLY"

OK, in baseball, that means don't chase any bad pitches. Have you swung at something ugly lately? Have you chased any bad *pitches*? These could be bad pitches or offers from others or just bad ideas or expectations that you come up with on your own. In my work, I often find folks who are chasing bad pitches over and over again. They are either always trying to please others or trying to be perfect. Which *bad pitch* do you often swing at?

Do you try to do everything perfectly? Do you realize that perfection doesn't exist? Why would you chase the impossible? Chasing perfection keeps you forever in the *loser's bracket*. It's like swinging a 32 inch bat at a pitch 6 feet over your head. Take a look at your own expectations, at the *pitches* you are delivering to yourself. Are you swinging at something ugly?

On the flip side, let's take a look at the people-pleaser. Do you believe that you have to please everyone on your team? As a leader, are you always trying to reach consensus? Sure, consensus is nice to have, but sometimes you just have to go with your gut instinct, take the risk of hurting feelings or messing up, and push forward toward your goal anyway.

That reminds me of another lesson from the loser's bracket:

"I WON'T TELL YOU WHEN TO GO [STEAL A BASE]. IF YOU HEAR MY VOICE, I'M TELLING YOU TO COME BACK!"

In this situation, the third base coach was talking to his player on third base who attempted to steal home. As you can see the coach has left it up to the player as to when he decided to try to advance. If the runner saw the ball get past the catcher, he was free to try to steal home. If, however, the runner hears the coach's voice, he should immediately reverse his course and return to third base. Isn't that cool?

In this case, the coaches are encouraging their players to take risks. The players can take any chance that they want. Some will try to steal on almost every pitch. Others will stand comfortably on third base keeping their foot on the bag until the ball is safely hit. In either case, the player is free to do as he wishes and the coach is his safety net. Are you that kind of leader? Do you realize how empowering that approach is to achievement and success? It encourages innovation and creativity. It encourages risk taking. It encourages a team member to test him or herself and learn new skills.

On the flip side, what kind of player are you? Do you stand on the base waiting for another runner to force you to advance? Are you afraid of being called out? Or, do you steamroll around the bases, running over everything in your path (including your own team members who batted in front of you)? I guess the real question is, do you have a coach that you can trust? If not, why not?

"FOCUS. SEE THE BAT HITTING THE BALL."

Do you use mental practice to achieve your goals? Top-notch athletes do this all the time. They don't just use their imagination to create expectations and envision outcomes; they envision the process. They focus on the physical mechanics of standing in the batter's box, swinging the bat, and hitting the ball.

Do you know the story of Laura Wilkinson? She was a US Olympic Athlete participating in the ten-meter platform dive in the 2000 Summer Olympics in Sydney, Australia. In preparation for the games, Laura broke three of her toes and was unable to get in the water. However this did not deter her from "practicing." She sat on the platform and focused on each dive over and over – every twist, flip, and perfect entrance. When her toes healed in time for the games, what happened? Laura came from behind and won the Gold Medal! She focused on the process just like baseball players focused on hitting the ball.

What do you focus on over and over again? Many gurus advise people to visualize themselves reaching their goal and receiving the prize. What would have been different if Laura had spent her time only fantasizing about the outcome and not the process that would allow her to achieve it? She could have been sitting on the platform fantasizing about the Olympic official placing the gold medal around her neck, flowers being placed in her arms, the American flag being raised, and the US National Anthem being played. The mental experience could have been so real that real tears of joy may have been streaming down her cheeks. What would have happened when it came time to take action and actually perform her dives? Honestly, the dives probably wouldn't have earned her that Gold Medal. Her focus wouldn't have been on the process and her performance, and her 'practice' of receiving the rewards would've created pain instead of success.

Do you focus on and practice the things that *YOU* control? Or, do you imagine what life would be like if everyone would just listen to you and do things your way? Mentally rehearse the process and envision the actions needed to succeed. Go ahead, try it! And, while you're at it...

"TUCK IN YOUR SHIRT!"

It may seem kind of odd that I put this piece of advice in here, but I got to thinking about it and you know, being prepared and looking good can be important to your success. No one wants to follow a sloppy leader. Sometimes we are so focused on telling others what to do that we neglect to look in the mirror at ourselves.

Do that right now! Look at yourself. Do you look the part? Are you a leader you would want to follow? Do you look like a parent that a kid would want to listen to? Look at yourself. If you were your spouse or significant other would you want to... well, I won't go there, but you get the picture.

Let me encourage you to tuck in your shirt and look the part. As an umpire, our crew wears matching uniforms. Is it because we love wearing polyester pants? No. It's so we look the part. It would be much easier for a manager to argue a call and disrespect someone in shorts and a t-shirt. But, when you are wearing a pressed uniform of authority, you carry a little more weight.

"WATCH ME (THE COACH), NOT THE BALL. I'LL TELL YOU WHEN TO STOP."

Oh, you see it all the time when you watch Major League Baseball or other professional sports... the athletes who stand there admiring their work or doing a little celebration dance forgetting that they are in the middle of a job. Does that ever happen to you? OK, you probably aren't admiring your work *per se*; instead maybe you are criticizing or gossiping about someone else's work or lack thereof. Maybe you are too willing to allow interruptions or spend time doing unnecessary tasks.

Focus on running the bases. Filter out the interruptions and distractions. These are unnecessary speed bumps or road blocks that slow you down and distract you from running your bases and scoring the run.

THE LOSER'S BRACKET

I want to tell you what happened at the Texas East State tournament in 2009. In three of the age brackets, the team that came from the "loser's bracket" ended up beating the team from the winner's bracket *twice* and taking home the state title. That sort of makes the "loser's bracket" a misnomer, doesn't it?

Many times we allow others to put us in a "bracket" that *THEY* named. I want to encourage you to do as these kids did... don't allow minor setbacks to deter you from your goal.

- Keep practicing.
- Listen to your coaches.
- Focus on YOUR actions.
- Filter out interruptions and distractions.
- For heaven's sake, tuck in your shirt.
- And, never, ever give up on your dreams (even if someone says you're in the loser's bracket)!

119

You have what it takes to be a CHAMPION!

Section 5

Your Transformation

Back to School

For some people those words bring thoughts of joy and friendship, for others they bring thoughts of dread, teasing and getting up early. Truth is, though, life is school. Every day you have opportunities to learn.

So, my question today is: Are you in school today?

Ray Kroc of McDonald's fame once asked it this way: "Are you green and growing or ripe and rotting?"

Today's World

We live in an information-powered world and a knowledge-powered economy. If you're not continually upgrading your competence, your aptitude, your attitude, you are becoming obsolete.

Henry Ford once said, "If money is your hope for independence you will never have it. The only real security that a man will have in this world is a reserve of knowledge, experience, and ability."

So, regardless of what your bank account balance was a year ago, how does your *knowledge account balance* compare to this same time last year?

Let's take a look back and answer these questions:

- What have you learned over the past year?
- Did you plan on learning that or was it by accident or coincidence?
- Has that knowledge enhanced your life?
- Did you learn something new in each area of your life (your vocation, your recreation, your relationships, your health, your wealth, your spirituality, your internal growth and development, etc.)?
- Are you applying what you learned?
- Are you a better person today than you were a year ago?

If the answers to these questions aren't what you'd like, there's nothing to worry about. You are just taking an inventory of what "is."

THE GOOD NEWS

The good news is that the choices you've made in the past don't need to affect how you move forward. You can choose to look at lifelong learning as the dreaded homework assignment that never goes away. Or, you can choose to look at it as an essential strategy for living long and living well.

Learning does not take place in the box we call a classroom or in a conference room or auditorium. We learn more, we learn better, and we learn faster by doing and being actively involved.

So how will this 'school year' be different for you than the last?

Will you be committed to improving *YOURSELF* or just interested in improving your circumstances? To improve your circumstances, you will only need to learn the latest, fleeting tips and techniques. To improve *YOURSELF*, you will need to focus on learning the timeless principles of success.

YOUR LESSON PLANS

Every good teacher knows that he or she must plan lessons in advance so that the students will get the most out of their learning time. These lessons must include repetition, 'boring' tasks, and discipline. Why? Because the teacher is teaching a new habit.

Just because you are no longer in a formal school environment doesn't mean you shouldn't have your own lesson plans. Take the time today. *Yes, I mean, today!* Don't procrastinate! Set out your goals for this coming 'school year'. Here are a few questions to consider...

- What areas of your life are the most satisfying to you right now?

124

- What areas of your life are the most challenging right now?
- What timeless principles could you learn regarding *BOTH* of these areas to make *YOU* better?

THE SOLUTION

Step #1: Set Learning Goals!!

In his book, *The Greatest Salesman in the World*, Og Mandino states,

> *"Today I will multiply my value a hundredfold. And how will I accomplish this? First I will set goals for the day, the week, the month, the year, and my life. Just as the rain must fall before the wheat will crack its shell and sprout, so must I have objectives before my life will crystallize. In setting my goals I will consider my best performance of the past and multiply it a hundredfold. This will be the standard by which I will live in the future. Never will I be of concern that my goals are too high for is it not better to aim my spear at the moon and strike only an eagle than to aim my spear at the eagle and strike only a rock?"*

Step #2: Stick with your lesson plan even through the rough times.

Og goes on to say,

> *"Today I will multiply my value a hundredfold. The height of my goals will not hold me in awe though I may stumble often before they are reached. If I stumble I will rise and my falls will not concern me for all men must stumble often to reach the hearth. Only a worm is free from the worry of stumbling. I am not a worm."*

Step #3: Practice, Practice, Practice what you learn & never stop doing steps #1 and #2.

Again Og's words:

> *"As a child I was slave to my impulses; now I am slave to my habits, as are all grown men. I have surrendered my free will to the years of accumulated habits and the past deeds of my life have already marked out a path which threatens to imprison my future. My actions are ruled by appetite, passion, prejudice, greed, love, fear,*

environment, habit, and the worst of these tyrants is habit. Therefore, if I must be a slave to habit let me be a slave to good habits. My bad habits must be destroyed and new furrows prepared for good seed."

Replace your old habits with new ones...

"... for any act with practice becomes easy. Thus a new and good habit is born, for when an act becomes easy through constant repetition it becomes a pleasure to perform and if it is a pleasure to perform it is man's nature to perform it often. When I perform it often it becomes a habit and I become its slave and since it is a good habit this is my will."

CHANGING THROUGH EXPERIENCE

You've heard the saying "experience is the best teacher", right?

The great Roman leader Julius Caesar recorded the earliest known version of this proverb, "Experience is the teacher of all things." around 52 B.C.

In 77 A.D., the Roman author Pliny wrote, "Experience is the most efficient teacher of all things." (Sounds like he copied most of it from Mr. Caesar.)

What I think they really mean is most people learn more by doing than by reading or listening.

Would you agree with that?

If experience is the best teacher, then why did I spend all those years in school? Was it to gain knowledge or gain experience? Shouldn't I just have gone out and gathered lots and lots of experience?

If experience is the best teacher then why aren't those with the most life experiences the most successful?

Will Rogers once said:

"The trouble with using experience as your guide is that sometimes the final exam comes first, then the lesson."

Og Mandino wrote:

"In truth, experience teaches thoroughly yet her course of instruction devours men's years so the value of her lessons diminishes with the time necessary to acquire her special wisdom. The end finds it wasted on dead men. Furthermore, experience is comparable to fashion; an action that proved successful today will be unworkable and impractical tomorrow."

Do you agree with those statements?

So which is it then? Let's look at axiology first and then we'll take a peek at how neuroscience and the brain work to answer the question "Is Experience the Best Teacher?"

THE VALUE OF EXPERIENCE

Knowledge (thinking) lays the foundation for experience, yet axiologically knowledge is infinitely **less** valuable than experience. You see, knowledge is systemic. By definition, it only exists in your mind. Experience is extrinsic. You can measure it and you can see it. Something that is tangible is infinitely more valuable than something that only exists in your head.

So, experience is infinitely more valuable than knowledge. *But is it the best teacher?*

Because you have measured it, seen it, and experienced it, does that mean that you have learned from it? Of course not!

It is implied in the saying "Experience is the best teacher" that if you experience a lot, you will learn a lot. Now I'm **not** going to tell you that experience isn't a good teacher but it is only a good teacher **if** it brings about change.

A rich and wise man once told me, *"To know and not do is not to know."* Sure I was confused at first, but then I realized what it meant. For example, to say you *KNOW* you should exercise more and not DO it is exactly the same as not knowing you should do it. Why? Because the *knowledge changes nothing.*

Quoting Og Mandino again:

"My dreams are worthless, my plans are dust, my goals are impossible. All are of no value unless they are followed by action. I will act now. Never has there been a map however carefully executed to detail and scale which carried its owner over even one inch of ground. Never has there been a parchment of law however fair which prevented one crime. ... Action, alone, is the tinder which ignites the map, the parchment, this scroll, my dreams, my plans, my goals, into a living force. Action is the food and drink which will nourish my success."

Many folks that I talk with believe that their experience is important. They will say "I have 15 years of project management experience." Truthfully that tells me that they have been in the profession for 15 years but it tells me very little about their knowledge and abilities managing projects. You see, some have had the same one year of experience fifteen times over.

You may assume that because you have experience you also have learned from that experience. But, you have to *DO* in order to truly learn and grow (change) from your experiences. What have you *DONE* with your experiences?

CHANGING THROUGH EXPERIENCE

It's been said that Benjamin Franklin was a master at learning from his experience. He was number fifteen of the seventeen children in his family and the youngest son of his father, Josiah Franklin. Josiah wanted Ben to attend school with the clergy but only had enough money to send him for two years and his schooling ended when he was ten years old. How did he accomplish so much throughout his lifetime? How did he take advantage of all of his experiences?

Good questions, but first, let's look at you...

- What experiences have you had? In the last year? Last week? Last 24 hours?
- Did you learn from these experiences? Can you remember them?
- What are the common traits of the experiences that you learn from?
- Have these experiences been viewed as successes or failures?
- What can you do to better learn from your experiences?

To answer that last question, let's go back to Franklin for some of his methods which line up quite nicely with what we now know from neuroscience.

Daily self-reflection was a fundamental aspect of Franklin's life. He developed a list of thirteen virtues and each day he would evaluate his conduct relative to a particular virtue.

Changing through experience isn't simply brought about through the experience. Ben Franklin kept a diary of his daily events. He also believed in the virtue of *ORDER* and he created a scheme for his daily life. Read through his plan below...

SCHEME.	Hours.	
MORNING. The *Question*. What good shall I do this day?	5 6 7	Rise, wash, and address *Powerful Goodness!* Contrive day's business, and take the resolution of the day; prosecute the present study, and breakfast.
	8 9 10 11	Work.
NOON.	12 1	Read, or look over my accounts, and dine.
AFTERNOON.	2 3 4 5	Work.
EVENING. The *Question*. What good have I done to-day?	6 7 8 9	Put things in their places. Supper. Music or diversion, or conversation. Examination of the day.
NIGHT.	10 11 12 1 2 3 4	Sleep.

He started every morning by asking "What good shall I do today?"

He reflected ("looked over his accounts") during his lunch hour.

He ended every day in reflection by asking "What good have I done today?"

Neuroscientifically, these techniques positively reinforced his good behaviors. *He developed a habit of creating good habits!!* In order to change thinking and valuing habits and learn from your experiences, you must **A.C.T.!!** You must give *ATTENTION* to the experience. You must *CONCENTRATE* on what you would like to learn and you must do this over *TIME*.

YOUR NEXT STEPS

What should you do to make your experience count?

Here are 4 steps on getting value and producing positive changes in your life from your experiences...

1) **Record.** Spend time each day jotting down the things that you did, the experiences that you had. Did your mind just tell you that you don't have time for this? Then, you'll want to check out the FREE online tools that you can find for your computer, PDA, Smartphone, Tablet, etc.

2) **Reflect.** Once you've collected your thoughts and experiences ask yourself the question "What good have I done today?" Look for value in each of the three classes of value.

   - Did you come up with some great ideas (systemic) today?

   - Did you do great deeds (extrinsic)? Were you productive in reaching your goals?

   - Did you value another human being today (intrinsic)? Did you make a positive eternal difference?

3) **Replay.** For many, your systemic thoughts cause problems. You have developed thought habits over the years that tell you that your ideas are the best and that your expectations are completely reasonable and realistic. However, for most, that usually isn't the case. (Do you still believe that you can drive in rush hour traffic

and not be cut off?) Use the creative and imaginative powers of your systemic mind to imagine yourself performing the best steps and actions. Replay the events of the day in your creative mind.

4) **Rehearse**. Mentally rehearse the good things that you did and pre-hearse the good things that you will do or change for tomorrow. Practice, practice, practice. Then, go back to step one again tomorrow and ask yourself *"What good shall I do today?"*

I must warn you... sincere self-examination of your experiences is not an easy task. It requires attention. It requires a willingness to face your experiences including the successes and the failures. It requires you to concentrate on your actions. It requires you to recognize what you may have neglected in thoughtlessness. It leaves little room for blaming others and complaining about the events of the day. This exercise focuses you on the only person you can truly change in this world... *YOU!*

But, I must also tell you... *IT IS WELL, WELL WORTH IT.* (You may even get schools, roads, bridges, and companies named after you some day like Franklin did.)

Remember, it takes all four of these steps to bring about real, lasting changes. To change you must A.C.T. Focus on your natural thinking and valuing strengths. You are worth the effort! Those around you are worth the effort.

RESOLUTIONS AND CHANGE

Have you made any resolutions lately? Resolutions are all about change. I like to think of it as being all about *GROWTH*. (Change is more difficult and sometimes feared, whereas growth is a natural process of living.)

Have you struggled with your resolutions or commitments in the past? If so, we'll take a look at change (growth) together in this article and hopefully, you'll be able to implement the steps needed at the end to realize your potential in the coming months. Let's get started...

CHANGE IS HARD!

I bet you already knew that change was hard but I bet you don't know just how hard it is.

Change or Die

What if that was your choice? Really. I'm not joking here. What if you had to change or you died? I'm talking about life and death - *YOUR* life or death. What if a super-smart, trusted authority figure approached you and said you had to make difficult and permanent changes in the way you think and act or your life would end soon, would you be able to do it?

"Yes," you say?
Really? Try again.
"Yes!!" you say with more emphasis as if I didn't hear you the first time.

The truth is you are probably deluding yourself. You wouldn't change. Not if it was too uncomfortable or difficult.

Don't believe me? Let's look at the statistics:

Let's look at patients with severe heart disease who have undergone coronary bypass surgery, a traumatic and expensive procedure that can cost more than $100,000 if complications arise. About 600,000 people go through this procedure every year in the United States and another 1.3 million patients have angioplasties at a total cost of about $30 billion.

These procedures temporarily relieve chest pains but rarely prolong lives or prevent future heart attacks. Many patients could *AVOID* the need for repeat surgery or repeat chest pain, not to mention changing the course of their disease and adding years to their lives, simply by switching to a healthier lifestyle. Yet, *very few do.* Their lives are at significantly greater risk unless they exercise and lose weight, and they clearly see the value of changing their behavior. But, after just two years, *over 90%* of them don't follow through. Even though they *know* they have a very bad disease and they know they should change their lifestyle habits, for whatever reason, they don't.

There are people in the legislative and executive branches of the US government who preach about improving healthcare in the US. Yet, for the last 50 years, even with all the advances in technology and medical care, the US is still plagued by the same five issues that it had back in the 1950's. Eighty percent (80%) of the healthcare budget in the US - estimated to be $2.4 *TRILLION* dollars annually = 15% of our economy = over 50% of the US Federal Budget - is spent on these five issues.

If you could change these five problems, you would solve almost all of the healthcare issues here in the US. That's amazing, isn't it? So, what are these 5 issues? *They are all behavioral and VERY preventable...*

- Too much smoking
- Too much drinking (alcoholic beverages)
- Too much eating (including high calorie beverages)
- Too much stress
- Not enough exercise

Have you ever tried to change any of these things in your life? Are any of these things on your list of changes currently?

CHANGE IS PAIN!

Pardon me for a minute, but I'm going to talk to you about your brain so that you can understand why change is hard and why it is painful.

When you are using your active brain (prefrontal cortex) to think about new things, it takes a lot of energy. Your brain, however, likes to conserve energy so when you think the same thoughts over and over, your brain moves those thoughts to your habit center (basal ganglia). The habit center functions exceedingly well without conscious thought on any routine activity. Moving thoughts from the working memory to the habit center frees up your working memory for more thinking. It's a fantastic process.

Now, your habit center is operating on automatic much like the transmission in your car. It will shift among its thought patterns of deeply held habits for you without conscious effort. Trying to now change these deeply held habits requires your brain to work harder. You've now got to apply a lot more attention to your brain and use your prefrontal cortex which is physically and psychologically uncomfortable. Why?

Because of the second part of the equation... your brain is wired to detect "errors." (That is why it's much easier to criticize than praise.) "Errors" are perceived differences between expectations and actuality or reality. When your brain notices errors, there are intense bursts of energy that come from neural firing. These error signals are generated by a part of the brain called the orbital frontal cortex. Located above the eyeballs, it is closely connected to the brain's fear circuitry, which resides in a structure called the amygdala. So, when your behavior is contrary to your habit, your brain detects it to be in "error". There is a lot of activity going on in your brain - some of it you can actually "feel" in terms of muscle tightness, headaches, pressure behind your eyes and so on. These error messages grab your attention, and they can readily overpower your rational thought. It takes a strong will to push past these mental activities, but YOU can do it.

CHANGE IS POSSIBLE!

So, now you may be asking why I have spread such "cheerful" news to you in this New Year. Well, I've told you all the difficulties regarding making changes, but there is also a lot of good news.

YOU CAN CHANGE!!

Yes, it will be hard and yes, it may even be painful but that doesn't mean it isn't **possible**.

Of all the abilities that you have been given, the greatest is that of change. Think about it, no matter where you are in your life today, you can change for the better.

So, *where do you start?* All real, lasting change involves changing the way that you think, the way that your brain processes information, expectations, and perceptions. You will start by working on changing your thinking habits.

Now, many gurus out there emphasize focusing on your end-goal... that big dream that you want to achieve. (Let's say its losing 30 pounds.) Some will even tell you to put pictures of that dream around your house, on your bathroom mirror, and add a date to it as to when you will achieve that dream or goal. (So, that would mean you should put up pictures of a beach or swimwear or an article of clothing that you'd like to fit into.) ***DON'T DO IT!!*** Sure, you have to have a destination in mind, but it doesn't have to be constantly shoved in your face every day reminding you that you aren't there. That can be *VERY* frustrating (as you have probably already found out). Frustration can be a motivator but for *most of the population it is* NOT. In fact, for most of the population is does just the opposite. (Studies have shown that only 1-2% of the population is positively influenced by this 'cognitive dissonance'.)

Instead, try these steps today to get you going in the right direction:

1) **Focus on the little things**. Have you ever noticed that when something big catches your attention you stop to stare at it? You see a hot air balloon going across the sky or big machinery building a bridge. That is soooo cool! It is almost mesmerizing. Well, my friend that is exactly what can happen if you focus your attention on your big goal. You will stop, you will stare, and in the meantime, you will not be taking any action. Standing in the middle of the road watching the unusual 'big' event occurring won't get you closer to the event although it may get you run over by a moving vehicle.

So, *focus on the little things...* what should you do today or tomorrow to get you closer to your goal? If you're trying to lose those 30 pounds, don't focus on 30 pounds, focus on making the right choices for breakfast, lunch, dinner and snacks... focus on exercising a little more... focus on taking the stairs - even if just for a flight or two - instead of taking the elevator. Do the little things *EVERY* day.

Focus on the little things... Why not let at least one car per day cut in front of you (instead of racing to block them)? This approach can help you lower your stress. Why not wipe your nose on a Kleenex instead of your sleeve? Why not take your dishes to the sink instead of leaving them on the table? Why not put your dirty clothes all the way into the hamper instead of leaving them on the floor? Why not park in the first space you see when you go to the store or mall instead of trying to win the "I parked really, really close" (so somehow I'm better than the person who parked farther away) competition? This can help you get a little extra exercise.

2) **Make your decisions ONCE**. Do you realize how much time and energy you could save if you just made your decisions once? What does that mean? Well, let's look at the goal above of losing

30 pounds... if you decided today (and decided to decide only once) that tomorrow you were going to limit your caloric intake to a certain number (say, 1200 calories - 300/meal and 3-100 calorie snacks) and eat healthy foods, then tomorrow when you saw the leftover cookies and candy from the holidays, you wouldn't have to decide whether or not to eat them because you made that decision yesterday.

Or, let's say that you decide to get up 30 minutes early tomorrow morning to workout. Now, it's tomorrow morning and since you've already made the decision, when your alarm goes off you don't have to re-make it. When the alarm goes off, you just get up (regardless of how you "feel") and follow-through on your decision to work-out.

What would be different in your life if you just made your decisions *ONCE*? Can you imagine it? You've decided to do the little things, so when someone doesn't hold the elevator for you, you don't get frustrated or angry because you decided that you were going to take the stairs up a couple of flights and get the extra exercise.

3) **Learn to "Forgive" yourself and "Keep Moving"** in the direction of forming new, good habits. When did you start believing that you had to be perfect or that mistakes were "bad"? Many of my clients talk about their fear of failure or making mistakes. This year, embrace your mistakes! John Maxwell wrote an entire book on the subject: *Failing Forward: Turning Mistakes into Stepping Stones for Success*. You can't reach success without failing. Did you get that? You cannot possibly ever reach success without failing. So, don't fear it - embrace it.

Forgiveness is simply the act of *releasing an expectation* which is causing you to suffer. Expectations only exist in your mind. Instead of standing still and staring at the "big" mistake, put it into perspective... you can't do anything about it now except learn from it. Shift your expectation to a positive preference or position. This way you won't be frozen but will keep moving in a positive direction... focusing on the little things (that you can control) and making your decisions once.

Og Mandino says:

"In truth, the only difference between those who have failed and those who have succeeded lies in the difference of their habits. Good habits are the key to all success. Bad habits are the unlocked door to failure... As a child I was slave to my impulses; now I am slave to my habits, as are all grown men. I have surrendered my free will to the years of accumulated habits and the past deeds of my life have already marked out a path which threatens to imprison my future. My actions are ruled by appetite, passion, prejudice, greed, love, fear, environment, habit, and the worst of these tyrants is habit. Therefore, if I must be a slave to habit let me be a slave to good habits. My bad habits must be destroyed and new furrows prepared for good seed. I will form good habits and become their slave."

Practice these three simple steps and you will become "a slave to good habits." Habits that you consciously created by doing the right things every day.

ROLES ARE HOLES

Role playing is hard work. Have you ever noticed that?

Take a moment to observe how you interact with other people. You may detect changes in your attitude, behavior, and speech depending on who you are interacting with. When you talk to a child, or when you talk to a server in a restaurant, do you speak differently? How about when you talk to your boss or when you talk to the janitor? When you walk into a store or the post office or the department of motor vehicles you may act differently than when you walk into your home or attend your kid's ballgame.

Why is that? Well, simple... *you are playing roles*. You are becoming the person you think you should be in that situation. Your mind has developed an idea about how you should behave in the situation. In that case, you are NOT *being* you, you're *doing* you.

PLAYING YOUR ROLES

So, you might have just had the thought, "of course I act differently in different situations." You can't act like a teacher when you are a customer in the store. You can't act like you're the owner of the business when you're just an employee. You can't act like a project manager when you're the CEO. You can't act like a child when you're the parent. Of course we act differently in different situations.

Really? Why is that? Think about it. In each of these instances, why can't you just be you? Why do you have to *act* at all? Where do these expectations come from?

Many times you completely forget about your intrinsic nature, your being, because you are so focused on your extrinsic nature. How often do you see yourself as a *human doing*? You have this image or concept that your mind has created (or accepted) about how you should act in each specific situation in your life.

If you live in America or another free country, you should appreciate the freedom that you have to choose. You no longer live within a "class system." In civilizations where liberty is not a birthright, certain functions are allotted to certain people. You are a 'born' ruler, priest, warrior, farmer, craftsman, laborer, merchant, and so on. In a free country, your function in this world, which would have been a matter of your birth, does not have to be your role.

YOUR ROLE HOLES

Today social structures are less rigid and less clearly defined. Yet, you still create these roles in your own mind and firmly place yourself into them. What do these roles look like? Your roles can fall into a number of categories:

- **Functions**: As we've discussed, the role you choose can be based on the functions you fulfill. You can be a parent, a child, a sibling, a leader, a follower, etc.
- **Beliefs & Values**: The role you choose can be based on your beliefs... your religion, your political affiliations, the causes you support. You may be a Christian, Hindu, Muslim, etc. Or a Democrat, Republican, Libertarian, Independent. Or an animal rights activist, MADD member, 'green' supporter.
- **Emotional**: Happiness and "Just Fine" are roles that you may play. You hide behind a smiling, positive façade, while truly you feel discouraged, frustrated, or disappointed.
- **Circumstances**: You can find yourself playing the hero or the villain... the lover or the fighter... the victor or the victim.

In all of these instances, you are defining yourself through a role. Putting yourself in a hole that limits your 'being'. Your "role hole" can be the pit that limits your intrinsic (infinite) nature.

BEING YOU

As someone who umpires Little League baseball games, I have the privilege of seeing others identify themselves by their role during the baseball games.

There are *managers* who think that they are playing the role of Major League manager. When things go wrong, they'll criticize the umpires for making a bad call. Some will rant and rave along the dugout, make comments under their breath, stomp out onto the field in disgust. Is that really helpful in their function as a Little League manager? Nope. As a matter of fact, it's hurtful on many levels. But it sure helps their mind live up to the expectation of "manager."

There are *parents* who think that they are the protectors. Sure, part of the function of being a parent is to look after the needs of a child, prevent them from getting into danger. However, some parents become that identity and their sense of self is largely caught up in the role so they become overprotective. These are the parents that blame the umpire when little Johnny doesn't get the called strike. They tell Johnny that the umpire robbed him and that it wasn't his fault. Is that really helpful to Johnny or anyone else? Nope. As a matter of fact, it's hurtful. But, it helps them to feel good about living up to their mental image of how a parent protects their kid.

There are, of course, the 9 - 12 year old *players*. (Isn't that funny that we call them players and not participants?) These *players* are fulfilling their roles just as they've seen on T.V. They think that they have to spit, and be disrespectful to the umpires, coaches, etc. They go through the routine of their favorite Major Leaguer and try to act as one. They even throw their bats and helmets when they get called out on strikes. Is that really aligned with the purpose of their participation? Nope. But it sure does help them measure up to the expectation that was created for them in their own minds.

Oh, and of course, there are the *umpires*. They play the role of enforcer. Sometimes, they forget that it's kids that are participating, though. They make loud, obnoxious *"OUT"* or *"STRIKE THREE"* calls so that they "look" the part. They seem to overlook the fact that they just screamed into the face of a child and made them cry. Sure, they played their role, but was it really helpful? Nope. But, it sure did show that 9 year old how well Mr. Umpire could live up to the image of enforcer.

Can you fulfill the function of a parent, manager, player or umpire without *being* one? Of course, you can. You can just *be* YOU while *doing* those tasks.

The real, authentic *YOU*, is an infinite being. Sure, you perform various extrinsic jobs in your world which you can and should do just as long as, in your mind, you don't become or play that role.

When you *play* a role, you may not be being true to the person you were created to be. You are living outside of your integrity. *WHAT?* Did I just accuse you of not living with integrity?! Did your mind give you a thought like, "How dare you accuse me of such a thing? It's not like I lie, cheat, steal, or kill anyone."

Really? It's so amazing how creative our unobserved mind can behave... how deceptive it can be in its creation of assumptions about itself.

When you are untrue to *YOU* and your intrinsic nature, you are lying to yourself and those you interact with. You are disingenuous and only letting others see your make-believe self (that your role "requires" you to be.) You are cheating and deceiving others under an imaginary guise of self-protection or self-promotion. You are robbing and stealing your world of your infinite, unique, irreplaceable gifts by keeping them concealed behind the role's image that your mind thinks you should play. And, whether your mind will let you believe it or not, you have killed your ability to be *YOU* for that irretrievable moment in time.

CONSIDER THESE THINGS....

Which roles or titles in your life do you most identify with?

- Are you a business owner, corporate executive or leader that only identifies with your 'numbers' (your P&L, your balance sheet)?
- Are you a parent that finds your self-worth in the success or perceived 'goodness' of your kids?
- Are you an employee that only identifies with the dollar amount on your paycheck or the title on your desk?
- Are you the leader or manager that drives people to do more, more, more? Or is your identity wrapped up in being liked by everyone and avoiding conflict?
- Are you a spouse that keeps score? Should your partner be doing more things for you because you always do for them? Are they not doing their 'fair' share?
- Are you the good church-goer who has to be happy in front of the congregation? Do you pretend to follow the rules?

Newsflash: You are not your numbers! You are not a business owner, you own a business. You are the CEO, you lead a company. You are not your kids! You do, however, parent them. You are not your title! You are a person who performs the tasks of someone with that title. You are not your success! You are not the rules!

YOU ARE YOU!

The more you identify with roles, the more inauthentic you will be in your relationships. Did you get that? The more you identify with and define yourself by your roles, the more inauthentic you may be in your relationships.

When you are acting, you are inauthentic. Every role you play is fictitious. Through these roles, everything becomes distorted and corrupted by your mind-made "mini me" for whatever role you are playing.

If I may go back to my umpiring example... One of the things that I try to do when umpiring is be me. What does that mean? First of all, while I'm all dressed up in my spiffy uniform, I know that I am still a human being first. And, believe it or not, I make mistakes. Occasionally, if I make a bad call on a batter... say, I called a high strike that should've been a ball. The next time he comes up to bat, I might say, "Hey, sorry about that high strike last time. My bad." Why do I say that? Well, 1) because it's the truth, 2) because I want him to know that I know I made a mistake, and 3) I don't want him to swing at a bad pitch this time at bat because of my past mistake. I feel that to be true to who I am, I need to be fair to the batter. One might ask, "Doesn't that undermine your authority as an umpire"? Well, maybe, if I thought I was an umpire, but I'm not! I'm just umpiring... fulfilling that function. In reality, I've found that I am more respected and admired for being authentic than I ever would be for "acting like an umpire".

CLIMBING OUT OF YOUR ROLE HOLES

Are you able to see the instances in your life where you identify with your role instead of who are you?

Is it hard to separate who you are from your roles? Many people say they have a hard time *finding themselves*. They ask "How can I be myself?" Or they say "I don't know who I am." Is that you?

Knowing who you are is simply another expectation. Where did it come from? More importantly, how can you stop it?

Here are some helpful suggestions:

1) <u>Be aware of your roles and how you identify with them</u>. Are you fulfilling the function or living in the role hole? Are you limiting yourself by a wall of expectations based on tasks you are to perform?

2) <u>Give up defining yourself</u> - to yourself and to others. Sure, you can tell someone what you do, but don't say "I am a project manager" when what you really mean is that "I manage projects" or that your title is "Project Manager."

3) <u>Give up the expectation of 'knowing who you are'</u>. Learn to be completely comfortable with not knowing who you are. Your finite (extrinsic) mind will never be able to find the words to define the infinite (intrinsic) you.

4) <u>Understand that you are neither inferior nor superior to anyone</u>. True self-esteem, self-motivation and true humility come from that realization. Top leaders, as researched by Jim Collins in Good to Great, blend extreme personal humility with intense personal will (esteem).

5) Know that you are <u>most powerful, most effective, and most influential</u> when you are completely *YOU*.

When you think about all the people that you've actually met, whom do you admire the most? What traits do they have? In most cases, you will find that at the core, these folks are real, genuine and authentic. They are who they are regardless of where they are or what tasks they are performing.

What would your life be like if you could be the real *YOU*... real, genuine and authentic?

The Power of Focus

Many people avoid the process of setting goals altogether because of their own thoughts... thoughts that tell them that they somehow don't measure up. They feel that they know what they *should* do, but just don't do it. Do you know what your thoughts are telling you?

What is your FOCUS?

Have you been comparing yourself to an external ideal and saying "I'm not good enough" (or something negative like that) because you know you *should be* doing something, but you're not? Well, stop it! Don't fret over that. Let bygones be bygones. Make this year the year that you learn to understand and control your reactions to your own thoughts... the year you make your thoughts work for you instead of against you.

Let's FOCUS on the future!

What is it that you'd like to create for yourself in the 3 to 6 months? Next year?

Would you like...

- more success?
- better health?
- more wealth?
- better relationships?
- more clarity and balance?
- better leadership skills?

What is it that you'd like to focus on creating and achieving for your own professional and personal success in the coming months? Are you prepared to overcome the challenges that stand in the way of achieving your goals?

THE CHALLENGES OF FOCUSING

There are a couple of key challenges that you may stumble upon when it comes to focusing.

1) Choosing what to focus on
2) Maintaining your focus long enough to create real change

How many of your current goals are the same as your previous goals? From last month? From last year?

How many of your current goals will you abandon before the end of this month? The end of this quarter?

We all start out with good intentions, but good intentions never accomplished anything. Intentions are the "ready, aim" part of "ready, aim, fire." It isn't until we "pull the trigger" that we actually get things done. So...

- How do we choose which goals to focus on?
- Why is focus so hard to sustain?

YOUR KEYS TO UNLOCKING YOUR FOCUS

The key element of being successful in reaching our goals is to be sure to focus on the *habits* that will help us to become the person that we want to become.

Here are four key points about focusing:

1) **Concentrate your attention on the things that you DO want in your life** - don't focus on what you don't want. For instance, focus on "becoming healthier" or "running a 5k" instead of "losing weight" or "quitting smoking." (When you focus on "weight" and "smoking", even with the "losing" or "quitting" in front of them, you still use and reinforce the neural pathways needed to think about those things - thereby, actually strengthening the bad habit.) Work towards your goals and good habits (instead of trying to erase the bad ones).

2) **Focus on the process not the outcome**. If you focus on the outcome, you can easily become frustrated with your progress. Og Mandino says,

"The prizes of life are at the end of each journey, not near the beginning; and it is not given to me to know how many steps are necessary in order to reach my goal. Failure I may still encounter at the thousandth step, yet success hides behind the next bend in the road. Never will I know how close it lies unless I turn the corner."

3) Which leads to... **Set daily goals that focus on the tasks** that you need to accomplish each day to reach your goals. This way, if you miss a day or two, it isn't a disaster to your plan. You'll simply be able to get back on track again tomorrow by choosing to focus on that day's goals.

4) It's not just how hard you focus, but also how often and how long you focus... **Accountability enhances the consistency** of focus. Why do corporate executives, business owners, professional athletes and other top performers have coaches? Haven't they already reached the peak of their profession? They know a secret... that their coaches help them achieve their goals by offering a fresh perspective, advice and accountability. Why don't you try hiring a coach this year?

THE SCIENCE OF FOCUS

Our brains are like road construction companies. They love to build paths, roads, highways and superhighways (neural pathways). Your brain takes thoughts that it thinks regularly and creates roadways so that the next time you think the thought it has an easier path (using less energy).

Creating the first roadway uses your working memory and takes a lot of energy. As you keep focusing on the thoughts over time, those roadways go from dirt roads to alleys to highways and move to your thoughts to your habit center forming your habits. (Just like most drivers, your thoughts always want to take the easiest route.)

So, the objective to changing your behavior and reaching your goals is to form good habits and create the (neural) roadways that you choose to create and get you to where you want to go.

Focus our attention is all that is needed to create these roadways, move these thought processes and turn them into habits. (That focus can be conscious attention as well as sub- or un-conscious attention.)

NEWS FLASH: You have telekinetic powers!

What does this mean to you? In short, *you can change your physical brain by focusing your mind* and your thoughts. (It's real-life telekinesis - the ability of the mind to influence physical matter.)

If you focus long enough and hard enough, you will actually change the physical nature of your brain. Once this hardwiring is in place, you have moved through the *4 stages of learning* and developed habits.

Whatever your goals may be, a good coach can help you achieve them. *You are worth it!*

I believe in you. You can achieve your goals with focus!

CELEBRATING YOUR WAY TO SUCCESS

Setting, focusing and accomplishing your goals are great habits to form. However, there is another habit that will help you accomplish those goals even faster. It's the habit of celebrating.

CELEBRATION AND JOY

Have you ever watched children playing? Whether it's through competitive sports or just individually imagining and experimenting, it's really amazing to see the world through the eyes of a child. *They celebrate the little things.*

Recently I was able to witness a little girl in the airport pulling her *Dora the Explorer* roller bag to the gate. She arrived and said to her mom, *"Mom, I did it!! I carried my bag the WHOLE way!"* I also watched two little boys playing with a new truck. As one of the boys made the truck's siren go off, the other one said, *"You did it!! You did it!!"* My favorite occurred in San Francisco's airport where I witnessed a 3 year old little girl come running out of the restroom releasing her mom's hand and sprinting up to her dad in his nice suit and tie yelling, *"Daddy, Daddy!! I pooped!"* Oh, the joys of a nice bowel movement!

As kids, we celebrate any and almost every accomplishment. Then at some point in our lives, when we become "big" girls and boys and it's no longer "cool" to celebrate our successes we stop. Why is that? Why do we start to call those people that celebrate "big headed" or "self-centered" or "show offs" or "immature"? Why does celebrating take on a negative connotation?

Does another person's success somehow diminish our own? Is there a limited quantity of celebration in the world? Does their celebration somehow mean you don't get your piece of the celebration pie?

Have you ever wondered why "excessive celebration" is a penalty in the NFL and NCAA Football but you can rip off your shirt, slide across the field, and have your team pile up on you for scoring a goal in soccer? Why does it matter if they are *showing off*?

CELEBRATION AND YOUR BRAIN

Celebration is great for your brain.

Celebration has also been shown to lead to increased trust, communication, and risk-taking. Celebrating creates an atmosphere of optimism and hope. It focuses the brain on creating instead of avoiding.

Celebration releases chemicals called neurotransmitters at the synapses in your brain and these intensify motivation to act for more solutions and celebrations.

What are you reinforcing in your brain? Many of the clients I talk with are trying to "fix their weaknesses." They try to compensate for their shortcomings. By focusing on weaknesses, you are actually reinforcing that behavior in your brain. I want to encourage you the same way I encourage my clients - *STOP IT!!*

When was the last time you celebrated an accomplishment of yours? Celebrating your accomplishments equals *focusing on your strengths*. What your brain consistently focuses on are the thoughts and actions that eventually become your habits.

Og Mandino writes, "As a child I was slave to my impulses; now I am slave to my habits, as are all grown men. I have surrendered my free will to the years of accumulated habits and the past deeds of my life have already marked out a path which threatens to imprison my future. My actions are ruled by appetite, passion, prejudice, greed, love, fear, environment, habit, and the worst of these tyrants is habit. Therefore, if I must be a slave to habit let me be a slave to good habits."

MY CELEBRATIONS

What?? You don't have anything to celebrate?? That's not the truth! Let me give you examples of what I celebrated recently and how I celebrated.

- The large box of Q-tips that I bought at first appeared too big to fit in my drawer but it wasn't. So, I celebrated by doing a little *churn-the-butter dance.*
- I ate only 1/2 of my delicious lunch and brought the other ½ home. *Raise the roof!!*
- I called a kid out on strikes but it was only strike 2. Why did I celebrate a mistake? Because I was able to quickly forgive myself and joke about it to my fellow umpires. It didn't affect my next call or my self-esteem as it may have in the past. *Whoop whoop!*

Why does any of this matter? What habit was I trying to reinforce?

By celebrating the Q-tips, I'm encouraging my brain to take more chances. Go for the big box and hope it works out.

By celebrating bringing home ½ of a high calorie lunch, I'm teaching my brain to form good habits around eating.

By celebrating my self-forgiveness after a mistake, I'm teaching my brain to not be so hard on me.

YOUR CELEBRATIONS

What can you celebrate like a child today?
- Did you control your temper in a heated situation?
- Did you complete a task that you were procrastinating?
- Did you say "Hi" and smile at your neighbor or a total stranger?
- Did you step out of your comfort zone?
- Did you poop?

What can you celebrate like a child today?

As for me, did I mention that I've published a book?

Whoop!! Happy dance... cabbage patch, electric slide, churn-the-butter! Sparkle fingers and sparkle fingers with a big gymnast dismount finish! Ta-da!!!

Section 6

Moving Forward

IN SEARCH OF INFINITE VALUE

In business, we focus on strategy, vision, ideas and planning (especially as we start a new month or quarter or year). Then, we switch and focus on execution, tasks, and priorities. We focus on achieving tangible results: increasing sales, retaining talent, increasing stock prices, etc. Often times the important intangibles, like higher morale, motivation and commitment are overlooked.

We as individuals tend to do the same in life. We compare where we are today to where we were a year ago. We look at our paycheck, our car, our house. We compare these to our family members and friends and co-workers. Then, what do we do? We make grand plans to do more and have more by the end of the upcoming month, quarter or year.

SCIENCE OF VALUE

In my study of axiology (the science of value and value judgments), the items we discussed above fall into 2 of the 3 classes of value - systemic and extrinsic.

- Extrinsic: Extrinsically valued objects exist in the common, public, sensory world of space and time that we share with others. We can see them, measure them. They are real and tangible. Examples are physical objects, tasks, the things that we do.

- Systemic: Systemic values do not exist in public space and time. They are not physical or perceptible things; they exist only as mental concepts constructed by our minds. Examples are ideas, plans, rules, procedures, expectations.

There is, however, a 3rd class of value that is clearly missing from the discussion above... Intrinsic.

- Intrinsic: Intrinsically valued objects are unique, priceless, and irreplaceable. They are infinitely valued. Examples are rare objects, treasured heirlooms, timeless principles (wisdom) and human beings.

NEW APPROACH

In this article I'd like to help you focus on the immeasurable, the invaluable, the intangibles... yes, even the emotional.

Why?

Because when you do, the extrinsic rewards and benefits of your actions will take care of themselves. As Og Mandino writes,

> *"I am prepared for wisdom and principles which will guide me out of the shadows into the sunlight of wealth, position, and happiness far beyond my most extravagant dreams until even the golden apples in the Garden of Hesperides will seem no more than my just reward."*

Did you notice that he didn't say "I'm prepared for actions and ideas which will guide me..."? What's more, the systemic part of your life will not be filled with stress, discouragement and frustration at the circumstances of life.

How?

You may have been told not to talk about certain topics in public and especially at work... things like politics, religion, and personal matters. Emotional or emotionally-charged issues don't belong in the workplace, right?

Wrong! You are an emotional being. You can't separate your extrinsic nature (your *doings*) from your intrinsic nature (your *being* and your *becoming*).

Now, I'm not suggesting that you go to work tomorrow and cry or become angry and express all of your emotions openly. What I am suggesting is that you don't fear or flee from your emotions or the emotions of others.

YOUR LEGACY (INFINITE VALUE)

Do you want to make real, lasting, legacy-building changes in your life? Then, don't shy away from feelings or passion - *HARNESS IT!*

FACT: When people don't feel emotionally connected, they hold back (on average) 40% of their cooperation, commitment, and productivity.

FACT: For every 1% positive increase in the corporate climate (emotional environment), there is a 2% increase in revenue.

You can be a powerful influence in your world this year. To increase what you have and become better at what you do, make the commitment to:

1) **Value the person FIRST!** Learn how to intrinsically validate the people in your life. That means setting your agenda aside and stepping into their world without the need to be right, to fix them, to solve their problems. Learn to fully focus on others and their intrinsic, immeasurable value.

    "I will greet this day with love in my heart. And how will I confront each whom I meet? In only one way. In silence and to myself I will address him and say I Love You. Though spoken in silence these words will shine in my eyes, unwrinkle my brow bring a smile to my lips, and echo in my voice; and his heart will be opened." (The Greatest Salesman in the World by Og Mandino, Scroll 2)

2) **Connect with people on an emotional level.** Try this... when people ask you how you are doing surprise them and give them an honest answer. Quit saying *Fine.* Which definition of *fine* are you referring to anyway? of superior or best quality? a sum of money imposed as a penalty? very thin or slender? delicately fashioned? Stop saying *fine* - be original and honest and connect with the people around you.

    "I will greet this day with love in my heart. And how will I act? I will love all manners of men for each has qualities to be admired

even though they be hidden. With love I will tear down the wall of suspicion and hate which they have built round their hearts and in its place will I build bridges so that my love may enter their souls."
(*The Greatest Salesman in the World* by Og Mandino, Scroll 2)

3) **Invest in improving YOU, your intrinsic value** - who you are and how you think. Don't just look into improving your techniques or finding tips for manipulating your circumstances. Make real changes in YOU!

"I will greet this day with love in my heart. And most of all I will love myself. For when I do, I will zealously inspect all things which enter my body, my mind, my soul, and my heart. Never will I overindulge the requests of my flesh; rather I will cherish my body with cleanliness and moderation. Never will I allow my mind to be attracted to evil and despair; rather I will uplift it with the knowledge and wisdom of the ages. Never will I allow my soul to become complacent and satisfied, rather I will feed it with meditation and prayer. Never will I allow my heart to become small and bitter rather I will share it and it will grow and warm the earth."
(*The Greatest Salesman in the World* by Og Mandino, Scroll 2)

Intrinsic Faith vs. Intrinsic Fear

I'd like to talk to you about the properties and characteristics of success. As Og Mandino writes:

"Which two, among a thousand wise men, will define success in the same words; yet failure is always described but one way. Failure is man's inability to reach his goals in life, whatever they may be. In truth, the only difference between those who have failed and those who have succeeded lies in the difference of their habits. Good habits are the key to all success. Bad habits are the unlocked door to failure. Thus, the first law I will obey, which preceedeth all others is - I will form good habits and become their slaves."

Yes, "good habits are the key to all success." So, what good habits have you purposefully and consciously acquired lately?

Intrinsic Fears

In my studies of Dr. Robert Hartman's works in axiology, I came across his "twenty properties of the self-test" and I want to share these with you. He labeled these qualities "intrinsic faith" and "intrinsic fear." The qualities of "Intrinsic Faith" positively enrich our lives while those of "Intrinsic Fear" diminish us.

Let's take a look at his intrinsic fears. While we do this, I have purposefully not put them in a list format but rather added them throughout the text so that your brain won't skim through it. I want to encourage you to think about each property or characteristic. Yes, it would've been much easier to simply copy and paste his list, but please take the time to read through these. Consider these questions as you read through this list...

- Are you making excuses for your behaviors that match the intrinsic fears?
- Are your thoughts telling you that you don't 'fear' anything?

- Does one or more of these words stand out as thoughts/behaviors that you have frequently?

[1]Defiance and Spitefulness top Hartman's list. Do you ever feel [2]Aggressive or Defensive? Has anyone ever told you that you are overly [3]Competitive? Do you exhibit [4]Restrictiveness or Narrowness? How about [5]Cynicism which is a distrust of the integrity or intentions of others? Do you ever feel [6]Sanctimoniousness or Holier-than-thou? How about [7]Greed or [8]Vanity? Are you [9]Easily Hurt or Touchy at times? Even though you don't like to admit it, do you ever feel [10]Cowardice in the face of danger, difficulty, opposition or pain? At times are you [11]Vengeful and vindictive or [12]Heavy Handed? Hartman also lists [13]Complicated / Lack of Common Sense as an intrinsic fear. Do you ever have a sense of [14]Irrelevance / No Sense of Proportion? How about [15]Irrationality, [16]Systemic-ness or Rigidity? Do you ever feel [17]Tense or Frantic? Do you act with [18]Inconsistency, Hesitation or Impatience? Do you sometimes feel [19]Non-aware, Dull or Cold? Do you ever suffer from [20]Indifference or that "Whatever (insert eye roll here) attitude"?

IT'S A SMALL, SMALL WORLD

Here is an abridged version of Hartman's description of Intrinsic Fear...

People experiencing intrinsic fear and suspicion cannot trust the world, they can only trust themselves. During these moments, all they have is their own power. They have to be the ones who command for otherwise everything would go awry. They have and need a feeling of superiority and indispensability for they are the only ones who can make order in the universal chaos. In business these are the ones around whom everything has to circle. They cannot delegate authority. If they did everything would go wrong; in some instances they feel that the world itself would fall apart. They are the ones who keep it together, precariously, by its seams. The world view of those living in intrinsic fear is restrictive. Every building up of the other means a tearing down of him/herself. Thus, when they praise they have to do so with condescension so that their own merit will not be obscured.

Anything that goes against those with intrinsic fear is exaggerated because it is so unjust, and anything that goes for them is taken for granted. They will not venture, in either thought, feeling, or action beyond certain limits. Few things appear to be possible. They are only of the present, trying to conserve what they have rather than risking it in great enterprise. They are spiritual cry-babies, and it is this that makes them cowardly. The fearful are irrational. Their defective thoughts about their 'self' interfere with the clarity of their vision. They use systems and rules in order to bolster themselves and exert control over others.

Lastly and most importantly, the fearful, since they lack a sense of perspective, are indifferent towards what really counts, especially toward the infinite greatness of the human being. Since they are weak inside and hate to be touched by anything unpleasant, they are indifferent against suffering and have little or no compassion. To the fearful, the world is, indeed, a small place.

Can you see how these characteristics interfere with you being the best YOU that you can possibly be? Can you see how these properties, feelings, and thoughts are counterproductive to your success? When you exhibit any of these properties, you have no ability to intrinsically value others because your mind is giving you thoughts that **only focus on you** AND you are choosing to react and respond to them.

These types of thoughts are devaluing, not only to others, but to you as well.

INTRINSIC FAITH

So, let's look at what we should focus our minds on. Again I'll use the paragraph format.

Topping the Hartman's list is [1]Humility which is the modest opinion or estimate of your own importance, rank, etc. You should also focus on [2]Serenity and being peaceful, calm, or tranquil. [3]Cooperation, [4]Expansiveness, and [5]Humaneness are also attributes of those who live in intrinsic faith. How often do you feel [6]Magnanimous and [7]Generous? Are you understanding and tolerant of others (or only those who agree with you)? Do you focus on being [8]Unpretentious, modest, humble, open and easy-going? If you're living in faith, you are also [9]Not Easily Hurt; you are [10]Bold and Courageous. You are [11]Forgiving and [12]Gentle. You give others the benefit of the doubt even if you are offended. Another quality of intrinsic faith is genuineness - you exhibit [13]Authenticity, Purity, Innocence, and Common Sense. Do you understand your role in the world; your [14]Relevance and Sense of Proportion. Unlike those living in intrinsic fear, the faithful are able to be [15]Rational and reason effectively. [16]Spontaneity and Flexibility, being open to influence and change comes easy because of your [17]Relaxed Dynamic or calm and easy energy. Traits like [18]Perseverance and Patience come naturally because of your [19]Awareness, Vision, Warmth, and Wisdom. You know what is true or right and know just how to act. Lastly, as a person of intrinsic faith, you are completely capable of [20]Compassion and have the ability to step into another person's world and experience what they are experiencing.

IT'S A MAGNIFICENT, EXPANSIVE UNIVERSE

Here is the abridged version of Hartman's description of Intrinsic Faith...

The person of faith is aware, wide awake to everything the world has to offer. Those of intrinsic faith are optimists. They see that there are many bad things in the world, but they are flaws of the design, or the execution, these flaws are not its essence. The faithful are expansive. Their spirits are as large as the whole world and take in everyone. They are continuously in love with the world and with everything in it. The faithful want to widely open up their soul to take in every experience.

The spirit of creation moves in them. The faithful will never say a bad word about anyone. They always build up the other; always find something good in everyone. They see the infinite in everything.

Those who live in intrinsic faith possess boldness and courage. Nothing appears to be impossible, every problem resolvable, every deed achievable, every difficulty surmountable. They take everything in stride, never getting overly agitated either in failure or in success. They are well-balanced and poised. They never expect anything from the world but take whatever they receive as grace, as a gift from the world. The faithful, being grounded in the essence of the world, see the important as important and the unimportant as unimportant. They take the important seriously and value it accordingly, and take the unimportant not seriously and disvalue it accordingly.

The deepest trait of the person of faith is Compassion. They suffer with the sufferer. They can openly, genuinely, and authentically relate to the world and find success in it.

Are you attracted to people who demonstrate these characteristics in their everyday lives? We want to be around people who are real, genuine, authentic, and just have a natural love of life. Do you sense these things in your life?

Can you see these traits and qualities within you? Are you able to see how they are the foundation of your success, your joy, your happiness?

Let me ask you, *please think about this for a minute...* as you were reading the paragraphs on intrinsic faith above, what thoughts were traveling through your mind? Were you thinking of reasons NOT to agree? Were you looking for flaws or examples in 'real life' that contradict what you read? Did your mind just skim over the words without absorbing them? Or, were you able to take in the true meaning of each sentence and experience those ideals?

What is written about intrinsic faith are timeless success principles. They have worked for thousands of years. Is your brain telling you that they won't work for you? **Newsflash**: *YOU ARE NOT YOUR THOUGHTS!* You can choose to retrieve another thought from your mind at any time and purposefully, consciously think on things that will support you.

THINK ON THESE THINGS...

You have the power to choose. Follow these steps to increase your success...

1) <u>Read through the list</u> of Intrinsic Faith characteristics every day.
2) <u>Pick one or two of the qualities and focus</u> on their meaning in the context of your life.
3) Begin to <u>recognize times throughout</u> your day when you could've exhibited those ideals but failed to do so.
4) Work on <u>shortening the time</u> between when you made a mistake and when you noticed it.
5) <u>Purposefully choose</u> to demonstrate one or two characteristics throughout your day.
6) <u>Notice all of the positive changes in your life</u>!!

INTRINSICALLY VALUING YOU

Do you ever think about your intrinsic, infinite value? In today's world, you are taught from a very young age that your value isn't in *WHO* you are but it is in *WHAT* you do and *HOW* you behave.

In elementary school you are first taught all the rules... don't cut in line, don't write on the walls, and don't put gum in Suzie's hair. Then, you are taught reading, writing and arithmetic and graded on how well you learned it. You are *measured* almost every day in school with tests, quizzes and homework. Are you ever taught about the value of people? Is it any wonder that you only see your systemic and extrinsic value?

Come to think of it, how do you even know that you are intrinsically valuable? Are you priceless and irreplaceable?

I tell a story at some of my speaking engagements... Those of you who are over 25 years old may remember the story of Baby Jessica. Baby Jessica was 18 months old when she was playing in the backyard of her aunt's house in Midland, Texas. Her aunt went into the house to answer the phone. When she came back moments later, the other children she was babysitting were looking down the casing of an abandoned well. As we later found out, Jessica was wedged in the 18-inch wide pipe 22 feet down. For 58 hours, the world watched as an estimated 450 volunteers tried to rescue 'Baby Jessica'. Drillers, miners and volunteers from as far away as Albuquerque, N.M. selflessly dropped everything and rushed to where their skills were needed.

Why? Why were so many people involved in the rescue of one little baby girl? Can you imagine how much money was spent drilling that parallel shaft and then trying to find a way to dig over to where the little girl was stuck? I mean, we didn't even know if Jessica was going to amount to anything. Was she going to do well in school, complete her homework and get stars on the top of her quizzes and tests? Was she going to behave and obey the rules? Really! Was she going to be worth all of this effort when we didn't even know what she was going to DO when she grew up? Besides, couldn't her parents just get together and make a new one?

OK, I am being quite facetious. *Why did we rescue her?* Because as long as those listening devices were picking up Baby Jessica's cries and sounds from that well, we all knew that there was *a precious human life* to be saved. No matter what the cost in materials or how many human labor hours were needed, as long as she was alive, our efforts to get her out would be unceasing. *Baby Jessica is a priceless, irreplaceable, infinitely valuable human being and so are YOU!*

DISTORTING REALITY

Over the years, through your experiences, your mind has picked up thought habits that do not accurately reflect reality. These thinking patterns were developed over time and now your mind *sees* the world through these distorted glasses. In some areas of your life the distortion isn't great at all. In others, the misperception and myths are truly detrimental.

MYTH #1: YOU ARE YOUR IDEAS.

At school and at work, you are judged on the value of your thoughts and ideas. As this continues to happen over and over and over again throughout each of your days, your brain may start to believe the *YOU ARE YOUR IDEAS.* Your mind may develop this habit and attach your self-worth (yes, your uniqueness, your pricelessness) to your ideas. When this distortion of reality happens, you may react in a number of ways. Let's see if you recognize any of these in your life...

- You may emphasize your dedication and commitment to what you believe is right or wrong. You validate your self-worth by making sure others know what you think. You may say things like "If I were in charge, I would _____." You may weave your beliefs and ideas into conversations to influence other people's opinions about YOU (as opposed to their view of situation that is being discussed.)

- You may let other people's expectations, opinions and ideas influence or even dictate your actions and decisions. In this case, you devalue your ideas and are more focused on pleasing others and gaining approval by pretending to agree with them.

- When others disagree with your ideas, you may become defensive or resentful, maybe even angry because their disagreement challenges or threatens you. When people say to you, "That is a stupid idea." Your mind just heard them call YOU stupid. (Which, by the way, they did NOT do. They simply told you that they didn't like your idea, albeit in a tactless way.

- Or, when others disagree with you, you may not stand up for your ideas giving others the impression that you are open, tolerant, or even agree with their ideas. Your mind will tell you that it is safer to agree than risk confrontation or rejection.

In each of these instances, if you believe that you are your thoughts, you may react to these thoughts and sabotage your success. You may sacrifice your integrity (being true to you) because your mind is distorting your reality.

FACT #1: You are NOT your ideas or expectations!

Your ideas can be worthless and ridiculous, but that doesn't mean that you are worthless. On the other hand, your ideas can be genius and pure brilliance, but your true value is still enormously more than that of your ideas. You can fail to live up to your expectations and the expectations of others, but that doesn't mean you are a failure. Your value is *SOOOO* much more than that of your ideas... axiologically speaking, *YOU* are infinitely, infinitely more valuable (∞∞).

MYTH #2: YOU ARE WHAT YOU DO

Everything we do these days seems to be measured or recorded or documented in some way. Then, it is compared to other measures. Your mind may develop the thought pattern that you are what you do and that your self-worth is based on how well you perform. When your brain creates thought habits that align your self-worth and self-esteem with what you *DO*, you will notice some of these things...

- You have to stay focused on your agenda. You must only do what you like to do. You may resent, resist or even refuse to do things that aren't personally fulfilling.

- You are pre-occupied with making a good impression. In this case, you are validating your self-worth through how you appear on the outside and the things that you accomplish. It really matters to you that people notice the way you look, your positional title, your possessions, your accomplishments, and even your talents and contributions.

- Your plate is always overflowing with tasks to perform. You feel the need to prove your worth by volunteering for tasks even though your schedule is already full. You are always meeting the needs of others, you can't say "No", and you don't make time for yourself.

- You compare your worst performance, talent, skill, accomplishment, etc. to someone else's very best. You have unrealistic expectations about what you need to *DO* for your own self-acceptance. You feel that your self-worth must be earned.

In each of these cases, your mind sees you and values you for what you *DO* (or don't do). This thought habit starts out when you're very young and the adults around you ask, "*WHAT* are you going to *BE* when you grow up?" Do you find that to be an odd question? I do. "What" and "Be" are on two very different levels of your life. The question should either be "What are you going to *DO* when you grow up?" OR "Who are you going to be?"

FACT #2: You are NOT what you DO!

Look back at the Baby Jessica story. If she were valued for what she did, we'd have left her in the well. I mean, if she wasn't bright enough to stay out of there in the first place, how valuable is she?

Often, when you make a mistake, do you beat yourself up about it? When someone doesn't like your idea do you feel devalued? Let's now look at the truth.

REAL REALITY

You ARE YOU!

You are a human being... a human "becoming." (Did your teachers ever emphasize that in school?) There is nothing more important or more unique in this world than your BEING.

You are UNIQUE, PRICELESS and IRREPLACEABLE!!

Do you ever intrinsically value you? Do you know what that would look like?

Here are a few questions to help you out:

- Do you appreciate and honor how your ideas and opinions characterize you as a person?
- Are you comfortable with your ideas and expectations?
- Do you keep your actions consistent with your beliefs?
- Do you set appropriate boundaries? Are you able to say the word "No"?
- Are you able to see how your actions, talents, appearance, contributions and possessions characterize (but do not define) you as a person?

- Are you able to separate the real *YOU* from the ideas and tangible, measurable things above?

Here are some thoughts to ponder about your true reality and becoming the person you were created to become:

1) You are UNIQUE.

   There is value in all that is unique and one-of-a kind. As Og Mandino says in his book:

   "Since the beginning of time never has there been another with my mind my heart my eyes, my ears, my hands, my hair, my mouth. None that came before, none that live today, and none that come tomorrow can walk and talk and move and think exactly like me. All men are my brothers yet I am different from each. I am a unique creature."

   No one can duplicate your creations, no one can write your story. In truth, no one else has all of your abilities and talents.

2) You are DIFFERENT.

   You are a unique creature of nature. Og says that you are nature's greatest miracle!

   "Henceforth, I will capitalize on this difference for it is an asset to be promoted to the fullest. I am nature's greatest miracle. Vain attempts to imitate others no longer will I make. Instead will I place my uniqueness on display in the market place. I will proclaim it, yea, I will sell it. I will begin now to accent my differences; hide my similarities... different from all others, and proud of the difference."

3) Do YOUR Best.

   Many times you may compare yourself to others. How can you compare one unique, irreplaceable thing against another? Are not both infinitely valuable? Other's deeds, actions, appearances, accomplishments have no bearing on *YOUR* value. Place this quote from *The Greatest Salesman in the World* in your memory bank: *"To surpass the deeds of others is unimportant; to surpass my own deeds is all."*

4) <u>Invest in Yourself</u>.

You may spend lots of time and money learning the latest tips and techniques of your trade. Many are designed to help you manipulate your circumstances. Still others worked terrific for the person teaching you the material, but they are not *YOU*. These techniques may be antiquated or may only work for those who think like the creator of the technique. Invest your time and energy *NOT* in improving your circumstances and your external surroundings... Invest in *YOU*. Invest in becoming real, genuine and authentic. Invest in learning to live in integrity... being true to *YOU*.

5) <u>BE Yourself.</u>

No one else can be you for you. Be real, genuine and authentic. Don't shield yourself from this world. *WE NEED YOU!* There is nothing to fear. Once you see yourself as *INFINITELY VALUABLE*, priceless, irreplaceable, you will strive for all of the goals and dreams that were placed within you. Sure you are going to stumble along the way, but don't concern yourself with a fall. Everyone must stumble on the way to their goals.

"What do you want to be when you grow up?"

Seems like a simple question, right? Millions of graduates are being asked that question during this graduation season. (Most of them by their parents who want to be sure that they're moving out of the house and paying their own bills. :))

I speak to thousands of "grown-up" people every year and many of them don't know what they want to be when they grow up. Do you find it odd that we expect a 17 or 18 year old to know the answer as they graduate from high school?

The belief or expectation that this is a simple question to answer can often get in the way of actually answering it. *It's not a simple question!*

As I think about the question from my past (What did I want to be when I grew up?) I realize that I'd have to ask my parents and friends from back then because I really don't remember. I know in high school I wanted to coach sports. But then again, I thought I was pretty smart so maybe I should go pre-med in college. That made a lot of sense because those 2 professions are so similar... not! One difference that became abundantly clear to me is that as a college basketball coach I would get to pick my players and work with people I had hand-selected ... as a doctor, I wouldn't get to pick my patients. I also remember from before high school that one thing I was *NEVER* going to be was a public speaker. I turned down the nomination to be the President of the National Honor Society and instead became Vice President because as the President, I would have been required to give a speech. Horrifying!!

Part of the problem with answering this question is the question itself. The "what" and the "be" don't match up! The "what" is extrinsic... a thing, tangible, measurable. The "be" is intrinsic... immeasurable, ever-changing, ever-growing.

We really should be asking:

1) What do you want to do? AND
2) Who do you want to become?

These questions are more easily answered.

So, *WHAT do you want to DO?* Do you want to do something technical, something creative, something inspirational, something meaningful? What would that look like in your life? "I like to work with my hands." "I like to work with people." "I like to do accounting."

Now, I believe the more important questions are... *WHO do you want to BE?* or Who do you want to become? I've heard some people say "I want to become a multi-millionaire." "I want to become a teacher." "I want to become a CEO."

If these are in line with your thoughts, will you allow me to share another perspective with you? A multi-millionaire, a teacher, a CEO... these things are, well, things. They are titles. They aren't immeasurable, ever-changing, and ever-growing. Your mind is mixing up the "be" and "what" making it hard for you to decide or answer the question.

When you are asked "Who do you want to become?" the answer should be about traits, attributes, and characteristics that you'd like to enhance or acquire. Here are examples: I want to become inspirational. I want to be more compassionate. I want to be more frugal, accountable, sincere, genuine, real, agile, respectful, kind, trustworthy, consistent, disciplined, tactful, or confident.

You see, I think we like the extrinsic, tangible, well-defined things because they seem to be easier to plan out, measure, etc. Yet, in reality, they can also be the hardest to attain because they usually depend on other people agreeing with you that you deserve to do or have what you want.

In our coaching program, we don't teach you to go after the extrinsic. We believe that when you develop intrinsically, the extrinsic will come your way. You will rightfully deserve to have it. But, more importantly, what you develop intrinsically can *NEVER* be taken away from you.

So the questions to ask yourself...

1) What attributes, traits, and characteristics would you like to acquire or enhance to become the person you'd like to become? List these out! If you need help on possible attributes, go to http://www.breakfreeconsulting.com/attributes for a list from my website. Pick 3-5 that are really important to you.

2) How do you set goals around increasing, say, your confidence, sincerity, appreciation, or consistency? Here are some hints:

   a. These goals should be completely within your control to achieve. For instance, if you want to increase your compassion, you may want to volunteer for organizations that would require you to do that. You are in complete control of the time you spend helping others. Set measurable goals around the amount of time you volunteer. While you're there, concentrate on your thoughts and your compassion and how to further increase this attribute and habit. If you are scheduled to work at the food bank and you don't go, well then, you chose not to increase your compassion that day. Use your natural strengths to do better at the next opportunity.

   b. Don't set goals that aren't under your control. (OK, I know that's the same as above, but it's an important point.) For instance, many people set goals to have so much money by a certain time. If you are saving this money in the stock market or other investment accounts, you don't have complete control of when you achieve your goal. Because stuff happens in life, you may not even have complete control over how much you put money into your account. Focusing on the amount of money saved can actually distract you from saving if you feel your expectations aren't being met fast enough.

c.   You'll measure your progress toward your goals through your activity toward the traits and attributes. So, let's say you DO want a certain amount of money. We call that your "dream", not your goal. An attribute needed to get that dream may be consistency. So, how do you grow your 'consistency'? You set a goal that you will help you increase your consistency using your natural thinking and valuing strengths. Maybe you make a goal to do the dishes every evening using your strength and desire to serve others. You can measure this by counting the days that you do it. It's under your complete control to achieve this goal (unless you have people fighting to do the dishes at your house. ;) Every time you reach your goal you are gaining more of the attribute you'd like, using your strength, and becoming more of the person you'd like to become.

d.   Celebrate your achievements! In the previous paragraph I talked about doing the dishes every night to develop consistency. Many people wouldn't take that approach because it isn't aligned with the extrinsic, monetary goal. They would think that it made more sense to set a goal around consistently saving money. (But, if you haven't done that already, that might not be aligned with your strengths so, why would you start there?) Once you develop the trait, you can learn to apply it almost anywhere at any time. Start out with goals you can achieve! Rely on your strengths to achieve them. Then, when you achieve them, celebrate your success. Let your brain know that this is the new habit that you'd like to create.

3) What goals can you set today that will help you gain the attributes that will help you become a better you?

Focus more on the BECOMING than the DOING. Sure, you're going to DO in order to BECOME, but focus on the becoming. When you focus on doing the task, it can be frustrating, boring, and mundane at times. It can feel like a burden, a duty or obligation. *When you focus on the becoming, you are now motivated intrinsically to do that very same task.* It's no longer a burden, but a stepping stone to help you become the person you'd like to become. I encourage you to give it a try. Believe in yourself!

So, *"WHAT DO* you want to *DO* when you grow up?" and *"WHO* do you want to *BECOME?"*

PEACE ON EARTH

I'm writing this in December and that is the time of year when you tend to hear a lot of good tidings. "Happy Holidays" "Merry Christmas" "Season's Greetings" "Joy to the World" "Happy Hanukkah" And also the one good tiding that I want to talk about which is "*Peace.*" Do you ever find yourself wishing for more "peace"?

This topic has been on my mind lately because my clients have consistently mentioned it when talking about what our coaching program has meant to them. I'm not saying this to toot my own horn, but listen to what one client had to say:

> "All I can say is "WOW!" That person on the team who drove me over the edge - this coaching gave me the tools to solve. The beating my head against the wall because nobody would give the project the same priority - this coaching gave me the tools to solve. Those roadblocks that occur again and again in my projects - this coaching gave me the tools to solve."

And another client said this about the coaching program,

> "Unexpectedly, I have discovered that no matter what thought you are thinking or emotions you are feeling, they cannot harm your soul. To be able to realize that nothing can harm you is the most empowering result I have experienced. I hope that everyone comes to realize this in some way. Most importantly, my relationship with God has improved and I know He is helping me along the way."

It's through comments and recommendations like these that I realize I'm in the "peace on earth" business. So, now I ask myself how can I, in this time of peace, joy and happiness, help you to find your piece of peace?

WHAT IS PEACE?

The holiday season usually adds stress to our lives. It's supposed to be pleasant and joyful, but it seems that a lot of time is spent worrying about presents or events. Some folks are worried about their football teams making the playoffs (Go Steelers! ;-). While there should be joy there seems to be more stress. There are a lot of holiday stress triggers. Are any of the following causing you anxiety?

- Finances - especially in this economy
- Time and Priority Demands - too many things YOU want to do
- Physical Demands - all the extra shopping and socializing expectations
- Relationships - family misunderstandings and unmet expectations

With all of this stress, how can you find peace? Some folks look for it in the latest and greatest gifts. If you've ever been to an IT consulting firm's Christmas party (as I have), you'd come to believe that peace was found in a *Best Buy* gift card by the way that they all steal it in the "white elephant" gift exchange. Others try to find peace in an extra slice or four of pie. Still others may look for peace in the adult beverages that are abundant during this celebratory time. It's amazing to me how many people search for peace "out there." They think that peace and joy will be found in the purchase of the best gift. They teach their kids that it's all about the gifts too. How many of "America's Funniest Home Videos" are of ungrateful kids opening gifts they weren't expecting? As if peace, joy and happiness in life could be found in a wrapped cardboard box.

So, what is peace? One definition from the dictionary says peace is "freedom of the mind from annoyance, distraction, anxiety, an obsession, etc.; tranquility; serenity."

If that's true then where can you find peace?

WHERE ARE YOU LOOKING?

Where do you look to find your peace? Are you looking for it in your job, in your relationships, in your hobbies? As I write this, I'm reminded of the song "Let There Be Peace on Earth." Do you know that one? The opening lyrics are: "Let there be peace on earth And let it begin with me." So what's that "begin with me" part all about? If it's supposed to begin with you, where do you begin?

I work with clients who are consumed with or at least bothered by discouragement, disappointment, disillusionment, frustration, fatigue, fear, annoyance, anxiousness, or anger. I wouldn't say that there is much peace in those emotions, right? Do any of those currently resonate with you?

So ask yourself, are you looking to find your peace in the things that you do or the things you own or things you've created? If so, why? Isn't there more to this life than that?

PEACE ONLY EXISTS IN THE "NOW"

Those negative emotions from above don't exist if you live in the now. You see the answer is hidden in that little song:

Let peace begin with me
Let this be the moment now.
With every step I take
Let this be my solemn vow.
To take each moment
And live each moment
In peace eternally.
Let there be peace on earth
And let it begin with me.

When you choose to live in the now, you realize that peace isn't something tangible. It isn't "extrinsic" in its nature. It's *INTRINSIC*. It is part of *WHO YOU ARE*, not what you do or what you have. Our society places so much importance on *WHAT* you do and *WHAT* you have that you often lose sight of *WHO YOU ARE*. As a matter of fact, when I ask folks, "Who do you want to become?" many just sit silently. What kind of question is that? Let me tell you the kind of question that is... *It's the kind that will bring you peace as you learn to find the answer!*

You see, *YOU* are unique, priceless and irreplaceable... regardless of what you do, what you own or the value of presents you give or receive. *YOU* are the bomb! *YOU* are perfect. Oh, sure, sometimes your actions and behaviors aren't perfect, but that's because you've formed habits based on what others (teachers, parents, bosses, etc.) have told you is important. Yet, inside of you, you know that your title, your salary, your home, your car don't define *YOU*. Hence, these things cannot bring you peace.

STEPS YOU CAN TAKE "NOW"

Here's some advice to help you lower the stress now and throughout the coming year(s)...

1) Throw out the expectations: When a thought that is an expectation comes into your mind (good or bad), get rid of it! Why would you spend time living in the future or the past when the present is so much more real and enjoyable? Your expectations, when unmet, can cause a lot of grief and emotions. So, instead of focusing on who did or didn't do what, focus on today. If your mind is habitually measuring reality against your imaginary, only-exists-in-your-mind expectations, your disappointment and discouragement with reality is inevitable. *YOU* are the boss of your expectations. Change them or throw them away.

2) Live in the *NOW*: Do you even realize how much of your life you miss every single day? How much time do you spend worrying?

How much time do you spend thinking about what life would be like "if" or "when"? How much time do you spend trying to impress or pretend? None of that occurs in the *NOW*... in reality. Look around you right now. What do you see that you *LOVE*? (I'm sitting here in my office typing and I see all kinds of things that remind me of what matters most in my life - of who I want to be. For instance, I love that my hands can type this message as I think these thoughts. See, isn't that simple? You can learn to do it too.)

3) <u>Simplify your life</u>: Life isn't nearly as difficult as your mind may be making it out to be. Who cares if someone doesn't like the gift you gave them? It's not the end of the world. So what if you burnt the sauce for the Christmas raviolis? (Yes, I grew up in an Italian family... and Mom didn't burn the sauce it's just an example. See you soon, Mom!) Who cares if a strand of lights is burnt out on the tree or you forgot to send a holiday card to your favorite aunt? No one's life is going to be forever ruined because of any of these things.

4) <u>Just BE YOU!!</u>: Trying to be someone else or live up to others' expectations or perceived expectations is exhausting. Give everyone the true gift of *YOU* this Christmas. How awesome would that be? Oh, sure, your mind just gave you thoughts on why you can't do that, but those thoughts are probably lies. *YOU*, the real *YOU*, the human being, are perfect! There is not a more beautiful you on this planet!! Why don't you just share that gift with me and all of the other people in your life? You'll be surprised at how *PEACEFUL* life can be when you simply are.

Dr. Robert S. Hartman, the father of axiology, writes:

> *"Just to Be, in daily life, is [the] highest [level of] maturity. Also it is very powerful for it brings into play the infinity of your intrinsic*

self. To scramble around in the treadmill of extrinsic value is not only immature, it is inefficient. It shuts up your infinite powers and lets them lie idle. It prevents you from really Living."

You see, *PEACE* is in *LIVING*... really living in the *NOW*. Now is not for sissies! You have to have courage to throw away the thoughts, ideas, expectations and fantasies that are not adding value to your life! Give it a try. Let things happen while you make things happen and see how joyful life can be.

Find peace in *YOU*... *YOU* are totally awesome! How do I know? Because you are a unique, priceless and irreplaceable human being. I don't care what you did in the past - those are bygones. I don't care about what your expectations or the expectations of others' say you *should* do or how you *should* behave today. It doesn't matter. All that matters is that *YOU*, the real *YOU*, show up today in this world. When you have the courage to do that, not only will the world be better because of it, *YOU* will be too. Break free of your old thinking and valuing habits and start using the brilliance that is already within you.

I wish you peace, joy and happiness throughout your life. Remember that the only place to find this is within *YOU*!

MAKE A DIFFERENCE

I talk to thousands of people every year. During these conversations I often ask about their dreams and goals. It seems that no matter what they say, when it comes right down to it, what people truly want is to know that they have made a difference in the world.

So, how do you best make a difference? How do you best live? How do you best love? What can you do to make sure you leave a legacy and that your life mattered?

I think it comes down to choosing and refusing.

I REFUSE

Many people do not know how to say 'no.' Saying no is an important part of making a difference. You can't do everything. You can't live up to everyone's expectations. You can't meet everyone's needs. You also can't be perfect. (Sorry to bring that up if you're a perfectionist.)

What are some of the things that you should refuse?

- Refuse to wait for someone else to do what you feel called or driven to do.

- Refuse to allow your fears to keep you from moving forward.

- Refuse to act like someone else in order to impress others.

- Refuse to make excuses or blame others.

- Refuse to be a victim.

- Refuse to gossip and speak ill of others.

- Refuse to mindlessly go through the motions in the roles of your life.

I CHOOSE

You have the most amazing power on the planet. You have the power of choice. You can choose your responses to your own circumstances, situations and most importantly to your own perceptions of these circumstances. It is your response that you are always responsible for. You can choose to let the old programs of your mind control your behaviors, actions and ultimately your success or failure. Or, you can consciously choose to be at your best by using your best thinking and by making decisions which are aligned with the brilliance of who you are. How do you do that?

- Choose to become mindful.
- Choose to focus on *YOUR* strengths.
- Choose to develop *YOUR* habits.
- Choose to commit to your best.
- Choose to love.

ALWAYS DO YOUR BEST

Sometimes we are led to believe that always doing our best is impossible. It's only impossible if we are judging the quality of the results of doing our best. Please understand that there are many, many circumstances that are outside of your control that impact the *results* of doing your best.

I'm just asking you to commit to doing your part in "doing your best." Your best is never going to be the same from moment to moment. Everything is alive and changing all the time. So, your best will sometimes be of high quality and other times it will not be so good. When you get a good night's sleep and are energized and well-rested, the results of your best may be better than on the days when you are ill or exhausted. Regardless of the quality of your results, keep doing your best – no more or no less than your best. If you try to do more by comparing yourself to others and trying to do "their" best instead of "your" best, you will spend more energy than needed and in the end, it won't be your best. If you do less than your best, you will subject yourself to self-criticism, frustration, discouragement, guilt and regrets. You will punish yourself and turn yourself into your own enemy.

When you do your best, you will take action. You will be choosing to take action because it is a natural part of who you are.

You will be taking action out of love, not because you are expecting a reward or recognition.

When you do your best, you will be making a difference.

When you simply do your best, you will matter.

When you do your best, you will be bringing your unique brilliance and gifts to the world... and, my friend, there is nothing more that the world could ask of you and nothing more that you can offer to the world.

You will be "being" you and that will always be enough. You are always enough.

Albert Einstein once said, "Many times a day I realize how much my own life is built upon the labors of my fellowmen, and how earnestly I must exert myself in order to give in return as much as I have received." He also said, "We have to do the best we can. This is our sacred human responsibility." I believe that he just wanted to give his best and be his best to make a difference in this world. That is all that is expected of us.

My hope is that this book and free assessment will help you to start to peel away the layers of thinking and old mental programs that are in your mind which are not aligned with who you really are. I hope that you realize that you aren't broken and you don't need to fix you or your weaknesses. I hope that you will have the courage to unleash your gifts, your natural strengths, and become all that you were created to become – for you and for the world. If I may speak for the world, we need you. You can and do make a difference. You matter! I believe in you!

References

FREE ASSESSMENT

Discover the specific ways of thinking that you already possess that are brilliant and then learn the keys to unlocking that brilliance. Using your VQ (Value-judgment Quotient) profile as a starting point you will identify the thoughts that both get in the way of making the best judgments and the thoughts that can actually serve you in creating success in all that you do.

This 15 minute VQ profile measures your strengths and weaknesses in very unique way. After you have completed the ranking of two sets of 18 items, you receive your *FREE* "First Steps" VQ Profile Assessment Report via email.

Your report will not only provide you with the keys to discovering how your current way of thinking is influencing your choices and actions, it will also provide a few tips and tools to help you make better use of your strengths while eliminating the negative impact of your "weaknesses". You may be relieved to know that it is not about fixing you. The fact is you are not broken.

Your *FREE* "First Steps" VQ Profile Report will show you one (1) of your most important strengths, two (2) of your greatest challenges and three (3) steps to immediately take to use your new insights and knowledge.

To get started go to http://www.vqprofile.com/breakingfree. You'll be asked to enter your first name, last name, phone and email address, then you'll be taken to the first of 2 worksheets where you will be asked to rank the 18 items according to their value. Basically you'll put the best, most valuable item/statement at the top of the list and the worst item/statement at the bottom. The rest you will rank hierarchically from best to worst. When you have completed the first worksheet, you will be taken to a second list of 18 statements. Again, the statement that has the greatest value or is the best you'll put at the top and then rank them accordingly until the worst statement is on the bottom. Then you will click the link at the bottom of the list to complete the assessment. You will be emailed a PDF file of your results upon completing the assessment. The text of the email will provide information on next steps and how to best utilize the information presented to you in your report.

Remember, this report does *NOT* measure behaviors or personality (although the text will try to relate your thinking to actions and behaviors). Your report measures your thinking and valuing habits. You may or may not respond to these thinking habits. You also will not agree with everything in the description of each of your measurements. We ask you to pay attention to the information and descriptions that you do agree with and try to think of examples of how these thinking patterns *show up* in your life.

We, then, ask you to follow the steps at the end of the report to immediately start to put your results to use in your life. Remember, it's about focusing on your strength by learning to ask yourself your centering questions, so please be sure to read that part of your report that shows you how to use it in your life.

Here's to your success and happiness.

BIBLIOGRAPHY

Amen, Daniel G. Making a Good Brain Great: the Amen Clinic program for achieving and sustaining optimal mental performance. New York: Harmony Books, 2005. Print.

"Daily Routines: Benjamin Franklin." Daily Routines. N.p., 7 July 1930. Web. 1 Dec. 2011. <http://dailyroutines.typepad.com/daily_routines/2007/07/benjamin-frankl.html>.

Dweck, Carol S.. Mindset: the new psychology of success. New York: Random House, 2006. Print.

Edwards, Rem B. "The Basic Concepts of Formal Axiology." Robert S. Hartman Institute. N.p., n.d. Web. 5 Jan. 2012. <http://hartmaninstitute.org/Portals/0/html-files/Ch.1,RV&Va.htm>. Self-Knowledge, Values, And Valuations

Goleman, Daniel. Emotional Intelligence. New York: Bantam Books, 1995. Print.

Goleman, Daniel, Richard E. Boyatzis, and Annie McKee. Primal Leadership: Learning To Lead with Emotional Intelligence. Boston, Mass.: Harvard Business School Press, 2004. Print.

Hall, Kevin. Aspire: Discovering Your Purpose Through the Power of Words. New York: William Morrow, 2010. Print.

Hartman, Robert S. The Structure of Value; Foundations of Scientific Axiology. Carbondale: Southern Illinois University Press, 1967. Print.

Hartman, Robert S., and Arthur R. Ellis. Freedom to Live: the Robert Hartman story. Amsterdam: Rodopi, 1994. Print.

Mandino, Og. The Greatest Salesman in the World. New York: F. Fell, 1968. Print.

Maxwell, John C. Failing Forward: Turning Mistakes into Stepping Stones for Success. Nashville, TN: Thomas Nelson Publishers, 2000. Print.

Metcalfe, Dr. Ray. "Six Common Strengths of Elite Performers - LeaderSavers." LeaderSavers. N.p., 21 Aug. 2006. Web. 1 Dec. 2011. <http://www.leadersavers.com/2006/08/six_common_stre.html>.

Milton, John, and Maurice Kelley. Paradise Lost, and other poems. New York: Published for the Classics Club by W.J. Black, 1943. Print.

Rock, David. Quiet Leadership: Help People Think Better—don't tell them what to do : six steps to transforming performance at work. New York: Collins, 2006. Print.

Schwartz, Jeffrey, and Rebecca Gladding. You Are Not Your Brain: the 4-step solution for changing bad habits, ending unhealthy thinking, and taking control of your life. New York: Avery, 2011. Print.

INDEX

ABOUT THE AUTHOR

Traci Duez has spoken to thousands of people and at hundreds of events around the world teaching them how to create their greatest success. In 2006 she started her own company, Break Free Consulting LLC, so that she could coach, mentor and teach others how to use their best thinking and valuing habits to dramatically improve their careers, businesses, leadership abilities, and relationships. She presents her powerful information at seminars, in workshops, through coaching programs, and in keynote addresses. Her audiences have described her as practical, authentic, funny, entertaining, enlightening, and inspiring as she shares her messages on how you can measure your valuing habits and learn to shift to your brilliant ones that will lead you to create greater value and bring you your greatest success.

Traci grew up as the oldest (smartest and prettiest ☺) of four girls in Jeannette, PA (near Pittsburgh). She earned a bachelor's degree in chemistry from Case Western Reserve University in Cleveland, Ohio. That may lead you to believe she is a bit of a nerd. (You'd be correct.) She then entered the master's program at The Ohio State University in athletic coaching. Eventually, she spent seventeen years in Information Technology which may lead you to believe she's also a bit of geek. (You'd be correct there, too.) Today, she uses her knowledge, research, and experience to bring the new discipline of neuro-axiology to life.

While Traci was growing up, she had very little self-confidence yet was told by others that she was a natural leader. How could that be so? This dichotomy started her on a path for determining how to be a true leader inside and out. In 2004 she came across a science, of all things, that forever changed her view of leadership and personal development. This little known, but powerful, science of axiology (study of value and human value judgments) changed her life and her career path.

26821854R00110

Made in the USA
Lexington, KY
17 October 2013